P9-CJJ-747

CROSS STITCH
▪ PLUS ▪

Lindsey Fox ▪ Heather Sproat

David & Charles

Many thanks to everyone who has helped us,
with particular thanks to Claire, Frances, Paul, Jill,
Michael, Steve, Susan and Geoff.

A DAVID & CHARLES BOOK

First published in the UK in 1997

Text and designs Copyright © Lindsey Fox and Heather Sproat 1997
Photography and layout Copyright © David & Charles 1997

Lindsey Fox and Heather Sproat have asserted their right to be identified as authors
of this work in accordance with the Copyright, Designs and Patents Act, 1988.

The designs in this book are copyright and must not be stitched for resale.

All rights reserved. No part of this publication may be reproduced,
stored in a retrieval system, or transmitted, in any form or by any means,
electronic or mechanical, by photocopying, recording or otherwise,
without prior permission in writing from the publisher.

A catalogue record for this book is available from the British Library.

ISBN 0 7153 0605 7

Photography by Paul Winch-Furness
Book design by The Design Revolution
Printed in the United States

CONTENTS

INTRODUCTION

*In this, our first book, we introduce you to the joys of
combining cross stitch with other exciting needlework techniques.
By working through the projects we have designed you will be able
to develop your embroidery skills, creating some truly lovely pieces
of work which you will treasure for years to come.*

*All of the projects are based on beautiful cross stitch designs and
each chapter introduces a different needlework technique to
accompany it – beadwork, ribbon embroidery, counted satin stitch,
blackwork, Hardanger and withdrawn and pulled work. A basic
techniques section shows novice stitchers how to cross stitch and
how to prepare for and finish work, while each chapter has full
instructions on the stitches used and the skills needed, with
step-by-step instructions, clear charts and keys.*

*The projects in each chapter have been designed for all
levels of stitchers – beginners, intermediate and advanced.
By starting each chapter with an easy project we give you the basic
building blocks of the techniques. As you practice your stitching
you will produce a range of beautiful objects – from paperweights,
cards and scented sachets, to a watch strap and matching brooches.
In the intermediate projects, we aim to develop your skills, allowing
your confidence to grow along with the size of the project.
Some of the designs in these sections range from samplers and
exquisite slippers to a beautiful sewing case. In the advanced
projects we let you loose on the full glory of each of the needlework
techniques so that you can really get to grips with each of
the types of stitching and enjoy yourself even more.*

*We hope that you have as much fun and enjoyment
reading this book and completing the projects as we have had in
designing and making them. We are sure that you will find it a
valued reference and return to its pages again and again
to stitch the enchanting projects.*

CROSS STITCH ▨ MATERIALS AND EQUIPMENT

The projects within this book actually require the minimum of tools, equipment and materials. Those items common to all the projects are described in this section; those specific to the individual chapters are described there under Tools of the Trade.

FABRICS

There are two main types of fabric used for counted thread embroidery – block weave fabrics, such as Aida, and evenweave fabrics, such as linens. The block weave fabrics are probably associated more frequently with cross stitch although it is just as easy to use an evenweave fabric.

Aida Block weave fabrics such as Aida, are woven to produce a material made up of blocks of threads with holes in between, which are easily stitched through to produce neat and even cross stitches. Aida is available in many different colours and in counts ranging from 7–18. A 7 count Aida has 7 threads to the inch (2.5cm) and 18 count has 18 threads to the inch (2.5cm). The smaller the count, the less stitches per inch and therefore the larger the stitches produced and vice versa. The most common count of Aida fabric used is 14 count, which has 14 threads to the inch (2.5cm).

Evenweave These fabrics are different from block weave fabrics because, as their name suggests, they are evenly woven. The count of evenweave fabrics range from

18–35, the most commonly used one being 28 count. A 28 count evenweave is equivalent to a 14 count Aida, because the stitching is over two threads of an evenweave, thus you divide the count by two to find its nearest equivalent in Aida. Evenweave fabrics are available in a large range of counts, colours and compositions.

The name of the type of evenweave will depend on the composition of the fabric, whether it is 100% linen or a mixture of other fibres. Hardanger fabric is an evenweave, woven in such a way that pairs of threads are woven as if they were one thread. This adds stability to the fabric and makes it ideal for this type of embroidery where there is a large amount of cutwork. Hardanger fabric is available in a 22 count.

Any of the charts in this book can be used to stitch on a different count of fabric of your choice. You just have to remember that you will need more or less fabric according to which count of fabric you use.

THREADS

Stranded cotton Stranded cotton thread is a six-ply mercerised cotton and is available in a vast range of colours. The cotton can be separated into six individual strands and then recombined in as many strands as necessary for stitching. It is ideal for cross stitch as you can use from one individual strand to six combined strands according to

the count of your fabric. The larger the count of the fabric, ie, the more stitches per inch (2.5cm), the less strands you will need.

Coton à broder Coton à broder is a single-ply matt cotton thread that is available in six different weights. The weight that we use for the blackwork projects in this book is No.16. It is a fine thread and the full thread is used when stitching.

Pearl cotton (or cotton perlé) Pearl cotton is a 100% cotton and is not stranded but is highly twisted, producing the effect of shine and shadow particularly when stitched in blocks for Hardanger work. As pearl cotton is not slippery it makes fastening off very easy and it is also washable. It is available in different weights, the thicker the thread the lower the number and vice versa. Generally pearl cotton No.5 is used for Kloster blocks and pearl cotton No.8 is used for all the lacy and filling stitches.

Blending filament Blending filament is a fine metallic thread which is combined with a stranded cotton to add a shine or highlight to a stitch. The stranded cotton is separated into the correct number of strands and then the same length of blending filament is added and both are threaded into the needle. It is best to use a fairly short length of thread as this helps prevent tangling and stretching of the filament.

Shaded threads Shaded or space-dyed threads are dyed by a special process where the dye is dripped on at different intervals and in different colours. The colours are left to bleed together, giving a most unique effect. Because of the process no two threads are exactly the same. The range of threads that we have used are Caron Watercolours, a stranded thread made up of three strands which are separated before stitching.

NEEDLES

It is important to use the correct needle for the count size of fabric and type of thread used, as too large a needle will create a hole and the stitches will be too small.

Needles are made from metal so it is important that you care for them properly. They can rust and mark your embroidery, particularly if left in your needlework for a long period of time. In this book we use mainly two types of needle – tapestry and crewel – both are easily available in mixed-sized packets. If you are allergic to normal needles (or just fancy a bit of luxury), try a gold-plated needle.

Tapestry needles These are blunt-ended needles with a long eye for easy threading. They range from size 18–26 (18 is the larger). The thicker needles are used for fatter thread and the coarser woven fabrics; the thinner needles are for thinner threads and finer woven fabrics. A blunt-ended needle is used for most counted thread work, such as cross stitch, as the needle does not pierce the fabric and therefore does not break the fibres.

Crewel or embroidery needles These are sharp-ended needles, with relatively long eyes. They range from size 5–10 (size 5 being the larger.) These are used when you need to stitch where there isn't a hole in the fabric such as in ribbon work. They are also useful for fastening off intricate work such as pulled or withdrawn thread work. You may need one for an item that uses a different fabric for making up and finishing.

Beading needles These are special needles used specifically for beading. They are very long and thin and so are ideal for threading small, fine beads.

SCISSORS

This is one of the most vital pieces of equipment in embroidery, however, it need not be one of the most expensive. You will need a pair of small, sharp scissors for accurately cutting threads and a larger pair for cutting fabric. Remember that all embroidery scissors go blunt after continual use so replace them regularly. Always try scissors before you buy them – they should be comfortable to use.

HOOPS AND FRAMES

We recommend using a hoop or embroidery frame for the projects in this book. This ensures that the fabric remains taut while you are stitching and so creates an even tension for the stitches. The frame you choose is a very personal one. There are lots of different types on the market and much depends on the design, the piece of embroidery,

and you. If you are a beginner it is a good idea to visit a reputable craft or embroidery shop and try several different types. There are two points to remember with regards the use of a hoop or frame. When stitching beadwork the whole design area should ideally be contained within the hoop or frame. When stitching pulled work make sure the fabric is extra taut and drum-like before stitching.

Embroidery hoops Embroidery hoops are portable, easy to carry and pack away quickly. It is a good idea to bind a wooden hoop so that it doesn't squash your stitches and holds the fabric firmer. Never leave your work in the hoop when you are not stitching.

Rotating frame This is a rectangular frame with round bars for the longest edges. These have fabric strips that you can sew your embroidery fabric on. The frame is tightened when the bars are rolled up and secured by nuts at the four corners. These frames are useful for larger designs.

Rectangular or slate frame This type of wooden fixed frame is not often used for counted thread work. The work is fixed by lacing and stretching with stitches or with drawing pins. The fibres must run true to the grain.

Flexi-hoop This is a plastic version of the embroidery hoop. It consists of two hoops clipped together to entrap the fabric and is ideal for small pieces. Finished work may also be displayed in them.

CROSS STITCH ▨ BASIC TECHNIQUES

CROSS STITCH

Cross stitch is worked in two stages, with two diagonal stitches worked over each other to form a cross.

1 ▨ Fasten on using a waste knot (see page 11) and then, following Figure 1, bring your needle up at the top left-hand corner of the square (1) and make a diagonal stitch, re-entering the square at the bottom right-hand corner (2).

2 ▨ Now bring the needle up at the top right-hand corner (3) and make another diagonal stitch, re-entering the square at the bottom left-hand corner (4).

3 ▨ If you wish you may make your stitches in the opposite direction, starting at the top right-hand corner of the square. Whichever direction you choose, it is important to remember that all the stitches must be the same, with the top stitch of each cross stitch facing in the same direction (see Figure 2). Some people prefer to make all the single diagonal stitches in one area before crossing them, however, we do not recommend that you use this method as over large areas the stitches can slip and give an uneven appearance.

4 ▨ When cross stitching on an evenweave fabric (depending on the count of the fabric) it may be necessary to stitch over two fabric threads. The cross stitch is completed in exactly the same way as if you were stitching on a block weave fabric such as Aida, but you count two strands of fabric before you put the needle back in (see Figure 3).

5 ▨ When stitching a row of cross stitches follow the order shown in Figure 2. If you chose to cross your stitches in the opposite direction to the one illustrated then you will probably find it easier to travel from left to right.

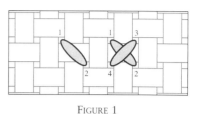

FIGURE 1

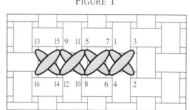

FIGURE 2

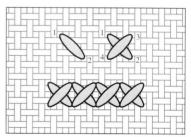

FIGURE 3

HALF CROSS STITCH

Half cross stitches (also known as three-quarter) are used to give extra definition. They are completed in the same way as whole cross stitches but one of the diagonals is half the length of the other (see Figure 5). Always make the smaller diagonal stitch first. Half cross stitches are just as easy to stitch as whole ones but can take slightly longer to perfect on a block weave fabric as you need to make a hole in the centre of the block.

1 ▨ Bring your needle up at the outer corner of the square and make a small diagonal stitch to the centre of the square. On Aida fabric you will need to pierce through the centre of the block weave, where there is no hole, with your needle (see Figure 4). On evenweave fabric you just make a diagonal stitch across one fabric thread rather than two. Finish the stitch by making the full size diagonal stitch across the top of the smaller diagonal (see Figure 5).

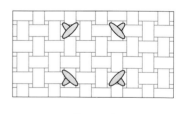

FIGURE 4

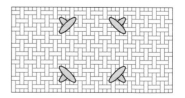

FIGURE 5

BACKSTITCH

This stitch, which can be worked horizontally, vertically or diagonally, can be used to outline a shape to give greater clarity or emphasis. Backstitch is one of the most common stitches in blackwork, used for both the outlines and the filling stitches. Full instructions for working this stitch are given in Blackwork Basic Techniques, page 72.

FRENCH KNOT

French knots work well with many types of embroidery, particularly cross stitch and ribbon work, producing an interesting, raised texture.

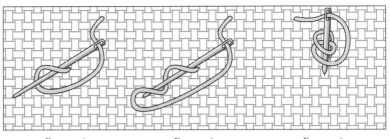

FIGURE 6A   FIGURE 6B   FIGURE 6C

1 ⊠ Fasten on the thread by passing it through the back of the cross stitch, then bring the needle up at the position indicated on the chart you are following.

2 ⊠ Place the needle under the thread and twist the thread around the needle as shown in Figures 6a and 6b.

3 ⊠ Put the needle back into the fabric, near the spot you brought it out (see Figure 6c). Pull the thread gently. This will form the shape of your knot around the needle. Pull the needle through the fabric very slowly, retaining the already formed knot shape, until all the thread is through. Don't pull too harshly or put the needle back in exactly the same spot you started from, or the knot will disappear through the fabric.

If you don't handle the thread firmly, you will get a floppy knot but if you pull the thread too tightly you will not be able to get the thread through.

4 ⊠ When all the French knots have been made, fasten off by making a small backstitch on the reverse of your work.

OTHER USEFUL STITCHES

Slipstitch This is a useful stitch, mainly used for neatly hemming and securing fabric.

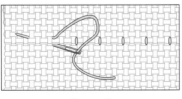

FIGURE 7

1 ⊠ Fasten on with two small stitches on the reverse of the work. Slide the needle through the fold or edge of the work and at the same time pick up a small thread of the fabric you want to attach (see Figure 7). Pull the needle through.

2 ⊠ Repeat this, making stitches ⅛in (3mm) apart. Space them as evenly as possible. Fasten off with two small stitches on the reverse of the work.

Blanket Stitch This is a useful and variable stitch, ideal as an edging. This stitch works from left to right and is not a counted thread technique.

1 ⊠ Fasten on by using a waste knot (see page 11). Take a stitch with the needle to the length required (this may be over the edge of the fabric). Wrap the

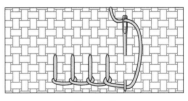

FIGURE 8

longer thread around under the needle as shown in Figure 8. Pull this through and repeat this to the end. The first stitch you take may appear strange, but as you stitch the row they will pull into shape.

2 ⊠ Try to keep the stitch widths and lengths even. Fasten off on the reverse of the work with a couple of small stitches.

CROSS STITCH PLUS ◙ BASIC TECHNIQUES

USING WASTE CANVAS

Waste canvas is used when working on a fabric base where the weave is too fine or not suitable for counted stitches, for example on satin or cotton jersey.

1 ◙ First make sure that the size of the waste canvas piece is sufficient to cover the area that you wish to stitch. Place the canvas over the selected area and pin it securely in place. Tack a central row of stitches across the canvas to hold it in place. All the tacking stitches should be about ½in (1.25cm) long and about ¾in (2cm) apart.

2 ◙ Tack a central row of stitches from top to bottom to create a central cross of tacking stitches.

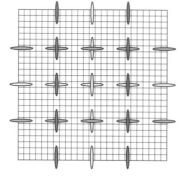

FIGURE 9

Tack the next two rows 1in (2.5cm) above and below the horizontal row of stitches. Tack a further two rows 1in (2.5cm) to either side of the vertical rows of stitches (see Figure 9). Repeat these tacking lines out from the centre until the whole canvas is secured by this tacked grid. Remove any remaining pins.

3 ◙ Using the waste canvas grid as a guide, begin to cross stitch as you would on a counted fabric. Once all the stitching is complete remove the tacking lines by cutting the ends and gently easing them out.

4 ◙ Trim the canvas to about ½in (1.25cm) of the stitching. Using a pair of tweezers gently ease out each thread in turn with a clean pull. Start working on the shorter threads first as this will make it easier to pull out the longer ones. The more you remove the easier this becomes. Some people prefer to dampen the canvas first to soften the fabric adhesive. This may be helpful on large areas of stitching but for small areas it is fine to keep it dry.

FINDING THE FABRIC CENTRE

Finding the centre of the fabric is important because this will relate directly to the centre of the chart, and is the place you normally start stitching. This will help you to check that the design will fit onto your fabric piece. The centre of your fabric is easily found by creasing it into four, lengthways then widthways. This point is then the centre and can be temporarily marked with a pin. Please note that some projects in this book recommend you start somewhere other than the centre; in these cases it is important make sure you have enough fabric to complete your design. If your design is large or worked on dark fabric, you may find it useful to stitch lines of tacking to use as reference to the chart.

MOUNTING FABRIC INTO A HOOP OR FRAME

It is advisable to use an embroidery hoop or frame to hold your fabric flat and taut when working. First neaten the edges of your fabric to stop them fraying, then find the centre of your fabric as described above.

If mounting your fabric into a hoop, sandwich the fabric between the hoops and tighten the nuts. Try to keep the fabric taut but don't stretch it out of shape. When using a rotating frame, mark the centre of the rotating bars and match this to the centre line of your fabric. Place the fabric under the strips then pin and stitch one side at a time. When you roll the bars the fabric will tighten automatically. If it is a large design you may need to lace across the side bars with extra stitches for more support. Covering your work with a clean cloth will keep it clean while you are not stitching.

USING A CHART

The charts for cross stitch in this book are made up of a grid where each square on the grid represents a square block of threads on the fabric and each symbol within a square represents a colour of thread. Use the key and project instructions to identify the symbols and the colour and number of strands of thread to be used. Follow the chart to stitch the design.

Refer to the individual chapters for any further instructions on chart use for the additional techniques. You can cross off areas of the chart, once you have stitched them, with a pencil.

FASTENING ON

Using a waste knot

At the beginning of a piece of work it is always best to fasten on using a waste knot as this keeps the back of the work as flat and neat as possible. First decide which block of stitching you wish to begin with, then thread your needle and make a small knot at the bottom of the thread. Insert your needle a little way away from the area to be stitched, about 1½in (4cm). Place the knot on the front surface of the fabric so that as your stitches fill the area they cover over the thread that runs under the fabric. (Place the waste knot in the path of the stitches.) When the stitches have secured this thread, the top waste knot can be trimmed and you will be ready to continue stitching.

Using a waste knot with a long thread

If threads on the reverse of the work need to be controlled, such as in Hardanger work, it is best to use a waste knot with a long thread. Having threaded your needle and made a small knot at the end of your thread, insert the needle through the front of the work about 4in (10cm) away from the area to be stitched. Place the waste knot away from the path of the stitches so that as your stitches fill the area they do not cover the thread that runs under the fabric. Once the stitching is complete, fasten off your stitching thread, cut the waste knot from the front of the fabric and re-thread your needle with the long end of the thread. Thread this neatly through the reverse of the work and trim.

Through the back of the work

If you are halfway through your worked piece and you wish to fasten on without using a waste knot you can do so by fastening on through the back of the work. Take your threaded needle and pass it through the back of the stitches about 1in (2.5cm) away from where you wish to stitch. Pull the thread through gently until the end of the thread disappears into the back of the work and then begin to stitch.

FASTENING OFF

Through the back of the work

If you have already completed a solid area of stitching and wish to change to a new colour you can fasten off by passing your needle through the back of the stitches on the reverse of the fabric, about 1in (2.5cm) away from where you made the last stitch. Once secure, trim the end.

A waste knot with a long thread

Once you have completed your stitching and fastened off your stitching thread, cut the waste knot from the front of the fabric and re-thread your needle with the long end of the thread. Thread this neatly through the reverse of the work about 1in (2.5 cm) away from where you made the last stitch, making sure that it is secure before trimming it.

Through the back of individual stitches

Some individual stitches, such as those used in Hardanger, need to be finished as neatly on the front as on the back. As Hardanger contains a lot of cutwork it is important that threads are fastened neatly and do not show through the holes. Once you have completed your embroidery, fasten off your stitching thread and cut the waste knot from the front of the fabric. Then re-thread your needle with the long end of the thread. Pass this carefully through the back of the individual stitches, making sure that it is secure before neatly trimming off the end.

CROSS STITCH PLUS
BEADWORK

This chapter is intended to have a floral feel, with beads used to complement the nature of the flower designs. By stitching beads on the flat, cross stitch embroidery is transformed into a three-dimensional medium, as the light catches the tiny glass beads, making the embroidery come alive.

Beadwork has a long history and since the earliest times beads have been used world-wide for adornment and decoration. Beadwork combined with embroidery became more popular after 1850, when charts of Berlin wool work began to include beads in their designs. The floral themes successfully used small beads to cover an area that once would have been stitched with wool, such as the shaded part of a petal. All Berlin wool work was presented on hand-painted charts – designs often employed clever use of shades of silver, grey, white and black beads and was known as grisaille work.

For cross stitchers it is amazingly easy to embellish cross stitch embroidery with beautiful beadwork. The symbols on charts representing a cross stitch can be effortlessly swapped to represent a bead, which is then stitched on in exactly the same area where the cross stitch would have been. Adding fine beadwork to cross stitch gives a rich, luxurious feel to your work, turning it into something truly special.

Originally, the finest beads came from France – the smaller beads called pound beads because they were sold by weight. Once beadwork had become popular they were made in Britain, but of an inferior quality. Today it is easy and satisfying to use beadwork in conjunction with cross stitch as the beads are easily available and are not too expensive. They are sold in small individual packets and the colour range is vast.

The projects in this chapter are functional yet beautiful and provide a solid introduction to beadwork plus cross stitch – beginning with simple areas of beads and working up to more complicated, large-scale designs which feature all the different techniques described.

BEADWORK 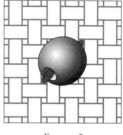 BASIC TECHNIQUES

SEWING BEADS ON DIFFERENT FABRICS

The construction of the various types of fabrics used for cross stitch plus beadwork will differ slightly depending on the fabric you choose. Generally though, the principles outlined in figures 1 and 2 will apply when sewing on beads. For a larger count fabric which has more threads to the inch, use a smaller size bead. For a smaller count fabric which has less threads to the inch, use a bigger bead.

FIGURE 1

FIGURE 2

Aida This fabric type is woven to form blocks of thread. Use half a cross stitch with a bead in the middle. This covers one block of the fabric (see Figure 1).

Evenweave For this fabric type use half a cross stitch over two fabric threads, with a bead in the middle. This covers a block of four fabric threads (see Figure 2).

SEWING ON A SEED BEAD

It is important in such fine and often detailed craft work to place your beads in the correct position and securely enough to withstand normal wear and tear. The beads used in this chapter are seed and bugle beads and they are sewn on after the cross stitch has been completed. The charts and keys will indicate where, and what, beads are to be applied.

1 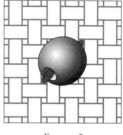 Begin by taking a length of fine, strong cotton thread in an appropriate colour and run this across a block of beeswax to make it even stronger.

2 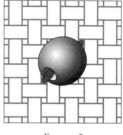 Using this thread and either a crewel needle size 10 or a beading needle, fasten on by taking the needle and thread through the back of a few of the cross stitches and secure with a tiny backstitch.

3 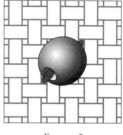 Bring the needle up at the position indicated on the chart you are following and thread the appropriate bead on to your needle. Make half a cross stitch and this will place the bead diagonally across the fabric (see

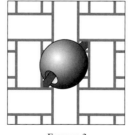

FIGURE 3

Figure 3). You should stitch the bead on in the opposite direction to the one you are travelling across the fabric (see Figure 4). The bead is then anchored securely with a loop stitch, as shown in Figure 5. Figure 6 shows the attachment of a succession of beads.

4 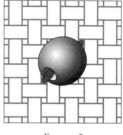 When the beading is complete, fasten off by passing the thread through a few stitches at the back of the work and secure with a couple of backstitches.

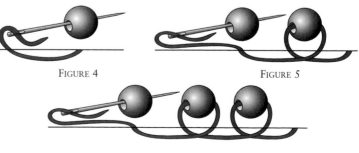

FIGURE 4

FIGURE 5

FIGURE 6

SEWING ON A BUGLE BEAD

Bugle beads are small glass tubes available in a variety of lengths and colours, making them ideal for embroidery.

1 ⊠ Begin by taking a length of fine, strong cotton thread in an appropriate colour and run this across a block of beeswax, to make it even stronger.

2 ⊠ Using this cotton thread and either a crewel needle size 10 or a beading needle, fasten on by threading through the back of a few of the cross stitches and securing with a tiny backstitch.

3 ⊠ Bring the needle up at the position indicated on the chart you are following and thread the appropriate bugle on to the needle. Take the needle back down through the fabric, either vertically, horizontally or diagonally (whichever direction the chart indicates) as shown in Figure 7.

4 ⊠ The bead is then anchored securely with a loop stitch in the same way as when sewing on a seed bead as described above.

5 ⊠ When you have completed all the beading, fasten off by passing your thread through a few stitches at the back of the work and secure with a couple of backstitches.

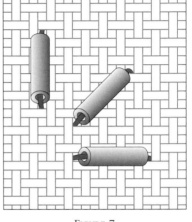

FIGURE 7

SEWING A SOLID AREA OF BEADS

To achieve a neat and secure result when stitching a solid area of beadwork, the beads need to be attached as described opposite but also be anchored with an additional thread. This helps align the holes of the beads and keeps them sitting in the correct position on the fabric.

BEADWORK STITCHING TIPS

• *Run the thread through beeswax to strengthen it, stop it fraying and to avoid tangles occurring.*
• *Dropped beads may be picked up by dampening your fingers.*
• *Make sure you always stitch your bead in the correct place. The symbols on the chart in this chapter either represent a cross stitch or a bead position. Look carefully at the keys to determine which it is.*

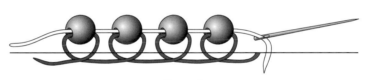

FIGURE 8

1 ⊠ Sew the beads on, as described previously. Then, starting at the edge of a block of beads, fasten on at the back of the work as before and pass the thread diagonally through the beads in a row (see Figure 8 above). The thread should travel through the back of the work and then down the second diagonal row of beads, and so on (see Figures 9 and 10 below).

2 ⊠ Repeat this until all the beads in an area have been threaded twice in this way.

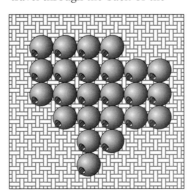

FIGURE 9

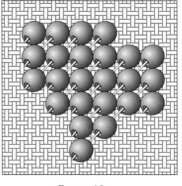

FIGURE 10

SEWING ON SCATTERED BEADS

In some cases a design calls for beads to be sewn on to fabric in a scattered or individual manner, with spaces between each bead. To ensure that your beads remain in the correct position carefully follow these instructions.

1 ◪ Attach a bead as described in Sewing on a Seed Bead on page 14. Before you sew on the next bead do a small backstitch on the back of the work to secure the first bead.

2 ◪ To sew on a bead some distance from this first bead, take the thread under a stitched area to where you want the next bead to be. If the thread shows through to the right side, fasten off and start again. The thread may jump the equivalent of six stitches but if it has to travel further, pass the thread under the stitches at the back of the work (see Figure 11). This ensures that the beads remain under the correct tension and that you will not be left with a long floating thread.

3 ◪ Sew on the next bead in the same manner.

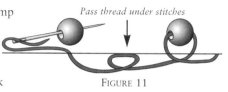

Pass thread under stitches

FIGURE 11

BEADWORK ◪ TOOLS OF THE TRADE

BEADS

There are many types of bead available today – in fact the choice can be quite bewilderingly wide. The beads described here are some of the more common ones used with cross stitch.

Glass beads Sometimes known as rocailles, these are the most popular to use with cross stitch. They are small, regular in shape and come in a vast range of colours and finishes.

Plastic beads Some people find these inferior to glass beads, however they are more hard-wearing and thus have an advantage. They are also cheaper generally.

Bugle beads These are long tube beads resembling small pieces of pipe. They are available in three sizes – small, medium and large – and in a wonderful variety of colours.

Antique beads Mill Hill produce a range of antique beads which are the same size as glass beads and can be used with them to give a lovely matt feel to your work.

Petite beads These are a smaller version of the glass bead and create a wonderfully delicate look to your finished piece.

FABRIC

Any fabric suitable for cross stitch can be used for beadwork. Remember though that if you are going to sew beads on an unstitched area make sure the beads won't get lost in the fabric: you must scale the bead size up or down according to the fabric count.

NEEDLES

There are special beading needles available which are very long, sharp and thin. They are ideal for very small beads, but if you find them awkward, try using a size 10 crewel needle.

BEESWAX

If thread is drawn across a block of beeswax before you start to use it to sew on the beads, it makes the thread stronger and less likely to wear against the beads and snap. Waxing also helps to prevent the thread twisting and knotting.

OTHER TOOLS

Small flat boxes Place a small piece of felt in the bottom of a small box and it will hold your beads so you can see to pick them up individually for sewing.

Small pots These can be used to store leftover beads. There are special storage pots available on the market or you could simply use small jampots.

Bead 'nabber' This is an inexpensive plastic thimble with an area of Velcro attached, allowing you to pick up dropped beads.

~ SCISSORS CASE ~

SIMPLY BEADS

*The scissors case makes
a beautiful as well as a
functional gift, while the
brooches and watch strap are
particularly lovely as the
beads catch the light when
moved. The techniques in this
section are simple to master,
particularly as the designs are
quite small. Choose from
three projects, all based on a
delightful forget-me-not
design.*

MATERIALS

*14 count Aida in pale green, two
pieces 6in (15cm) square*

Stranded cottons as listed in the key

Tapestry needle size 24

*Crewel needle size 10 or a
beading needle*

*Packet of Mill Hill beads (01005)
in pastel colours*

Sewing thread to match

*Felt in the colour of your choice,
two pieces 6in (15cm) square*

*Iron-on Vilene, two pieces 6in
(15cm) square*

Snap fastener

*It is always a bonus to have
an object of beauty that is also
practical. This scissors case is just
that and its delightful design is
quick and simple to stitch.*

WORKING THE EMBROIDERY

1 ⊠ Referring to Cross Stitch Basic
Techniques, page 10, mount the
fabric in a hoop or frame and work
the cross stitch from the centre as
shown on the chart on page 20.
Use two strands of stranded
cotton for the flowers and leaves
and one strand for the stems.

2 ⊠ When the cross stitch is
complete, sew on the beads as
indicated on the chart (see
Beadwork Techniques, page 14).

3 ⊠ Once the embroidery and
beadwork is finished, wash the
work. Then press it carefully right
side down on a thick, fluffy towel.
Iron on a piece of Vilene to both
the embroidered and unworked
pieces of Aida.

4 ⊠ Take a piece of paper and using
a ruler draw a triangular shape
around your embroidery scissors.
Create a curved or rounded end
where your scissors points will go
(you could use a mug or similar
circular object to draw around to
get a neat finish). Now draw 3/8in
(1cm) extra all the way round the

shape to allow for seams. Use this
as your pattern.

5 ⊠ Using the paper pattern as a
guide, cut out two in felt, one in the
unworked Aida and one with your
stitchery on, taking care that the
stitching is in the correct position.

6 ⊠ With right sides together, pin,
tack then sew the two pieces of
Aida together, leaving the top (the
widest end) open. Trim the excess
fabric and clip across the corners,
then carefully turn through to the
right side.

7 ⊠ Pin, tack and sew the two felt
pieces together, leaving the top (the
widest end) open.

8 ⊠ Place the felt pocket inside the
embroidered one. Turn the raw
edges in at the top and slipstitch
together.

9 ⊠ Stitch on a snap fastener to
close the top. We added tassels as
decoration or you could sew on a
length of ribbon so the scissors
can hang around your neck
or be tied to your
work-basket.

~ BEADED BROOCHES ~

MATERIALS
Stranded cottons as listed in the key

Tapestry needle size 24

Crewel needle size 10 or a beading needle

Small piece of iron-on Vilene

FOR THE FRAMED BROOCH
14 count Aida in pale green, 4in (10cm) square

Packet of Mill Hill beads (01005) in pastel colours

FOR THE ANTIQUE-STYLE BROOCH
28 count Evenweave fabric in cream, 4in (10cm) square

Two packets of Mill Hill petite beads, pale blue (42017), and pale lemon (40123)

These two brooches use the same design but different fabrics and beads. The framed brooch shows how beads can enhance a simple setting. The addition of beads in the antique-style brooch recreates an evocative feeling of the past. See Suppliers page 127 for details of the brooches used.

WORKING THE EMBROIDERY
1 ☒ Referring to Cross Stitch Basic Techniques, page 10, mount the fabric in a hoop or frame and work the cross stitch from the centre following the appropriate chart (see page 20). For the framed brooch, use two strands of stranded cotton for the flowers and one strand for the stems. For the antique-style brooch, use one strand of stranded cotton throughout. Stitch the cross stitch over one thread.

2 ☒ When the cross stitch is complete, sew on the beads as indicated on the appropriate chart (see Beadwork Techniques page 14).

3 ☒ Once the embroidery and beadwork is completed, wash the work. Then press it carefully right side down on a thick, fluffy towel. Iron the piece of Vilene on to the back of the embroidery to strengthen it.

4 ☒ Follow the manufacturer's instructions on how to make up the brooch.

~ WATCH STRAP ~

MATERIALS
Strip of 14 count Aida in pale green

Stranded cottons as listed in the key

Tapestry needle size 24

Crewel needle size 10 or a beading needle

Packet of Mill Hill beads (01005) in pastel colours

A strip of iron-on Vilene

Strip of felt for backing

This delightful little forget-me-not design is perfect to decorate a watch strap. The design has been charted in two sizes, large and small – choose the size that best fits your wrist.

WORKING THE EMBROIDERY
1 ☒ Remove the watch strap and fastening and keep it in a safe place (it will be re-attached later when the stitching is complete).

2 ☒ Place the watch strap on the Aida strip and carefully tack all the way around it to record its shape and size.

3 ☒ Work the cross stitch following the chart on page 20. (As this project is so small, a hoop or frame is not required.) Use two strands of stranded cotton for the flowers and one strand for the stems.

4 ☒ When the cross stitch is complete, sew on the beads as indicated on the chart (see Beadwork Techniques page 14).

5 ☒ Once the embroidery and beadwork is finished, wash the work. Then press it carefully right side down on a thick, fluffy towel. Iron the piece of Vilene to the back

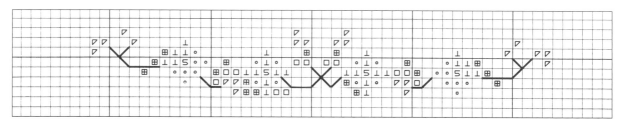

WATCH STRAP CHART (LARGE)

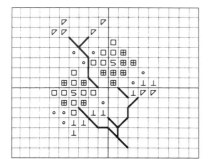

BEADED BROOCHES CHART

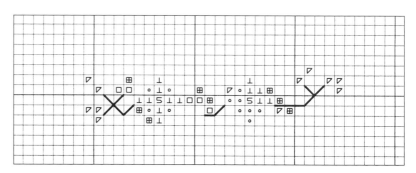

CHART KEY

	Anchor	DMC
∘	143	825
⊥	128	775
☐	244	701
⊞	239	703

Backstitch

▬▬	1014	355

S	Mill Hill Pastel Lemon bead
▽	Mill Hill Pastel Blue bead

of the embroidery for strength and trim down to size.

6 ▣ Carefully press the raw edges under. Glue a piece of felt to the back to neaten – you could slipstitch it in place to hold it even firmer.

7 ▣ Re-attach the watch strap fastenings back the way they were originally and then fix the strap to the watch.

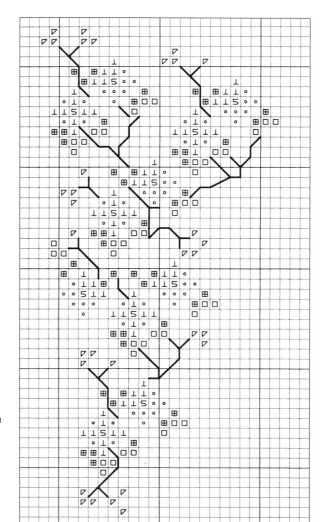

~ ROSE BOUDOIR DRESSING GOWN & CAMISOLE TOP ~

A SCATTERING

OF BEADS

This romantic collection of slippers, dressing gown and camisole would make a treasured gift for a bride. The items in the collection can, of course, be made singly but all give you plenty of practice at sewing on beads and introduce the additional technique of sewing on scattered and individual beads.

MATERIALS
Cream satin dressing gown and camisole top

9 count Zweigart waste canvas, two pieces 7 x 3¹/2in (18 x 9cm) and one piece 5 x 3in (12.5 x 8cm)

Stranded cottons as listed in the key

Two packets (about 16gm) of Trimits beads ('E' beads) in white

Tapestry needle size 24

Beading needle

Fine white sewing thread

This exquisite satin dressing gown and matching camisole top embellished with delightful rosebuds and dainty gypsophila capture a feeling of romantic indulgence. Using waste canvas to guide the positioning of the cross stitch and beads, this piece can be achieved quickly with stunning results.

WORKING THE EMBROIDERY ON THE DRESSING GOWN

1 ⊠ Measure approximately 7in (18cm) from the centre back seam of the collar on either side. Mark these points with a pin. Take the pieces of waste canvas and pin them on the collar so that they cover the area you wish to embroider – this should be approximately 7in (18cm) from the centre back seam on each side and close to the edge of the collar (see Figure 1).

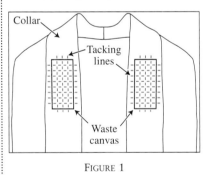

FIGURE 1

2 ⊠ Tack a central line through one piece of waste canvas vertically and then horizontally to hold it in place on the collar. Tack two more vertical lines about 1in (2.5cm) from the first line on either side. Repeat with horizontal lines on either side of the first horizontal line. A grid pattern of tacking should thus be formed which will hold the canvas securely on the

collar (see Figure 1). Repeat this grid-pattern tacking with the other piece of waste canvas. Remove the two pins.

3 ⊠ To start the cross stitch, find the centre of the waste canvas (by counting the threads) and, following the charts on page 26, use three strands of stranded cotton and a size 24 tapestry needle.

4 ⊠ Once the cross stitch is complete, begin the beadwork as indicated on the chart and using white sewing thread and a beading needle (see Beadwork Techniques page 14). Since the beads are scattered over the design it will be necessary to make large jumps from bead to bead (see Beadwork Techniques page 16).

5 ⊠ Once all the stitching is complete, remove the tacking and waste canvas threads (see Cross Stitch Basic Techniques page 10). Finish by pressing right sides down into a thick, fluffy towel.

WORKING THE EMBROIDERY ON THE CAMISOLE TOP

1 ⊠ Measure the centre of the front of the camisole and mark this point with a pin. Pin the waste canvas centrally on the top edge so that it covers the area you wish to embroider.

2 ⊠ Using the grid-pattern tacking described in step 2 of the Dressing Gown instructions, secure the canvas to the camisole top. Remove the pin. Continue by following steps 3–5 of the Dressing Gown instructions.

21

~ ROSE BOUDOIR SLIPPERS ~

MATERIALS

14 count Zweigart Aida in pale blue, two pieces 12in (30cm) square

Stranded cottons as listed in the key

Tapestry needle size 24

Beading needle

Packet of Mill Hill glass seed beads (00479) in white

Fine white sewing thread

Iron-on Vilene, two pieces 12in (30cm) square

Tapestry slipper kit (see Suppliers page 127)

These exquisite slippers are both beautiful, practical and easy to stitch. Decorated with blushing roses and delicate gypsophila, this design like the other in this collection was inspired by a type of Victorian posy called a tussie mussie.

WORKING THE EMBROIDERY

1 ▣ Referring to Cross Stitch Basic Techniques page 11, mount one piece of Aida in a hoop or frame and work the cross stitch from the centre, following the charts on pages 24 and 25. (The two charts are mirror images so the slippers make a pair.) Use two strands of stranded cotton and a size 24 tapestry needle. Repeat the embroidery with the other Aida square.

2 ▣ Once all the cross stitch is finished on both pieces of Aida, wash and then press the embroidery face down on a thick, fluffy towel.

3 ▣ Begin the beadwork as indicated on the charts, using the white sewing thread and a beading needle. Since the beads are scattered over the design it will be necessary to make large jumps from bead to bead (see Beadwork Techniques page 20).

MAKING UP

1 ▣ Once all the stitching and beadwork is complete, strengthen and stabilise both pieces of embroidery by ironing on the squares of Vilene. Take care not to squash the stitches or break the beads by ironing right side down on a thick, fluffy towel.

2 ▣ Take the printed canvas from the slipper kit and trim around the slipper outline provided with the kit 1/2in (1.25cm) from the edge. Using the cross stitch chart as a guide, tack a line around the outside edge of the embroidery, then trim to 1/2in (1.25cm) from the edge.

3 ⊠ Place the corresponding piece of canvas under each of the embroidered slipper pieces and tack, then stitch along the printed line. This will leave both pieces of embroidery backed with canvas in readiness to make up into a finished pair of slippers.

4 ⊠ Trim the canvas a further 1/4in (0.5cm) and push it inwards, towards the centre of the back of the embroidery. Following the printed guideline at the toe of the slipper, pinch the fabric together, tack, then sew along this line. This gives the shape of the toe.

This romantic collection of slippers, dressing gown and camisole top, would make a treasured gift for a bride.

5 ⊠ The embroidered Aida is now fully prepared and you can follow the slipper kit instructions on how to make it up into the slippers.

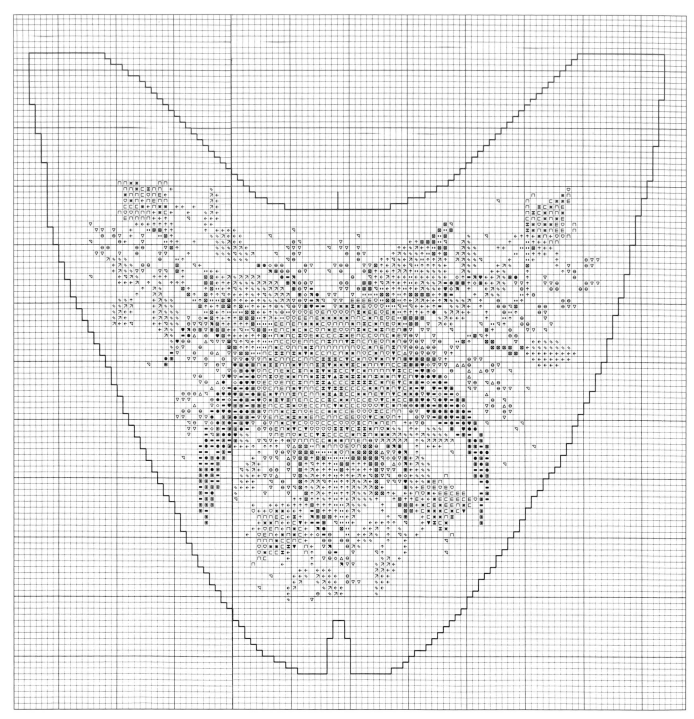

Rose Boudoir Slippers Chart (Left Foot)

Chart Key

	Anchor	DMC			Anchor	DMC			Anchor	DMC
▽	261	368		◣	255	907		••	879	500
⊖	876	502		◸	256	906		▽	330	947
△	877	501		←	239	703		E	334	606
▬	278	472		↑	227	701		⊓	46	666
◙	280	733		⊠	228	700		✻	47	321

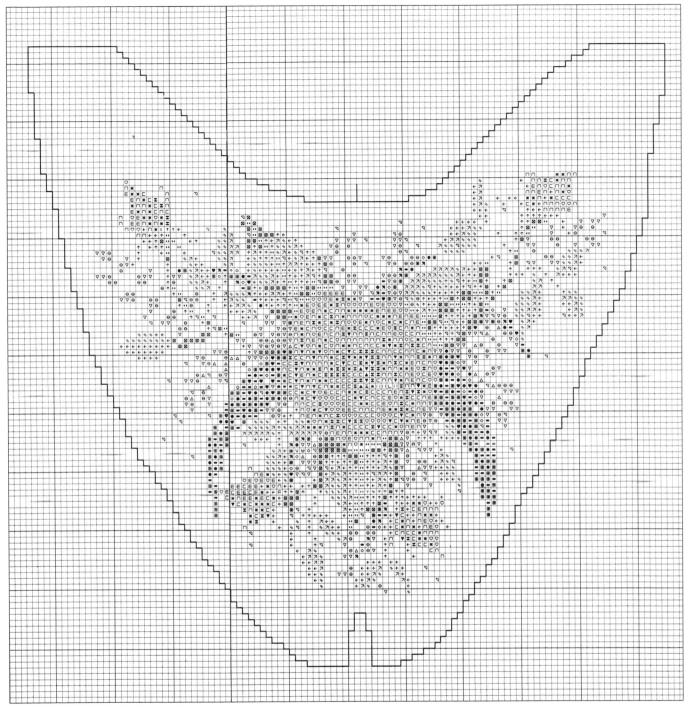

ROSE BOUDOIR SLIPPERS CHART (RIGHT FOOT)

	Anchor	DMC			Anchor	DMC
⊏	44	815		♥	290	973
⊠	72	814		◇	289	307
▼	102	550		●	292	3078
▲	178	791		◺	Mill Hill glass seed bead – white 00479
◤	291	444		—	Slipper edge

CHART KEY

	Anchor	DMC
▽	261	368
▬	278	472
▣	280	733
∥	255	907
◥	256	906
→	239	703
↑	227	701
⊠	228	700
▪▪	879	500
▽	330	947
∃	334	606
⊓	46	666
✳	47	321
⊐	44	815
⊞	72	814
▼	102	550
♥	290	973
◇	307	397
●	292	3078
▿	Trimit white 'E' bead	

ROSE BOUDOIR DRESSING GOWN CHART

ROSE BOUDOIR CAMISOLE TOP CHART

~ ORCHID PICTURE ~

BEADS AND ALL

This large project combines all of the beading techniques you have learnt in this chapter, allowing you to perfect them in this adventurous but gorgeous piece. There are no new techniques to master but the scale of this project makes it an exciting challenge.

MATERIALS

28 count Zweigart Cashel Linen in cream, 24 x 18in (61 x 46cm)

Stranded cottons as listed in the key

Beads as listed in the key

Tapestry needle size 24

Crewel needle size 10 or a beading needle

Sewing thread to match beads

The bugle beads around the edges of the petals are a perfect match for the flecks which occur on real orchids and an area of seed beads, such as on the leaves, gives a dense, waxy feel.

WORKING THE EMBROIDERY

1 ◼ Neaten the edges of the piece of linen to prevent it fraying too much. You could oversew the edges if you like.

2 ◼ Mount the linen in a frame and work the cross stitch from the centre of the design (see Cross Stitch Basic Techniques page 10) following the chart on pages 28 and 29. Use two strands of stranded cotton and a size 24 tapestry needle and stitch over two threads.

3 ◼ After the cross stitch is complete, work the backstitches (see

Cross Stitch Techniques page 9), using one strand of stranded cotton and a size 24 needle.

4 ◼ Begin the beadwork as indicated on the chart and using matching thread colours and a beading or crewel needle (see Beadwork Techniques page 14). Where there are solid areas of beadwork see the instructions in Beadwork Techniques page 15. Where the beads are scattered over the design it will be necessary to make large jumps from bead to bead so refer to Beadwork Techniques page 16.

5 ◼ Once all the stitching is complete, wash and carefully press your work, right side down on a thick, fluffy towel. It is now ready for stretching and framing (see Framing page 126).

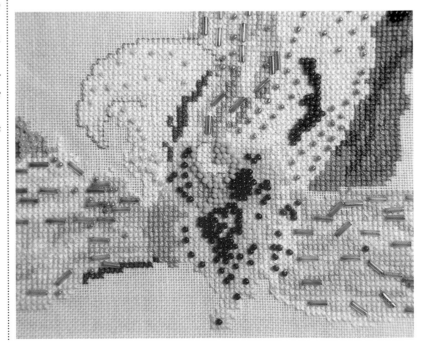

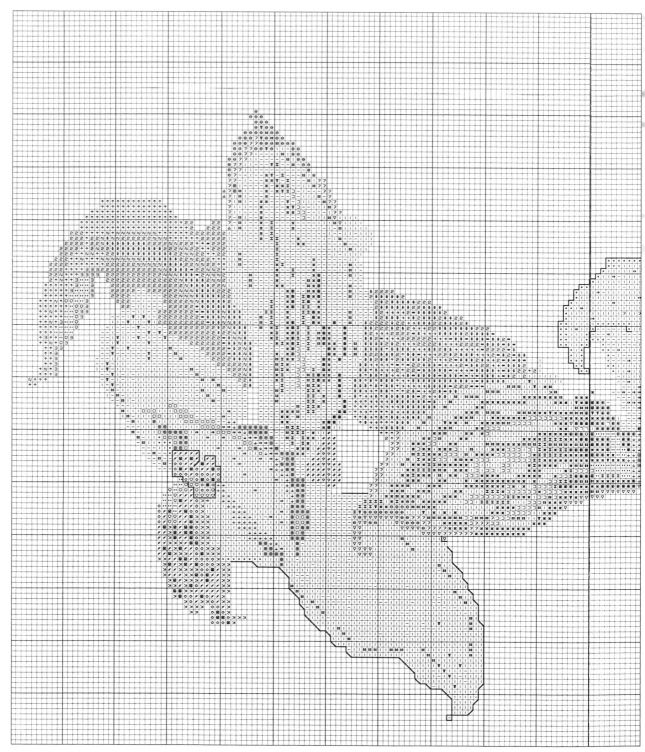

ORCHID PICTURE CHART

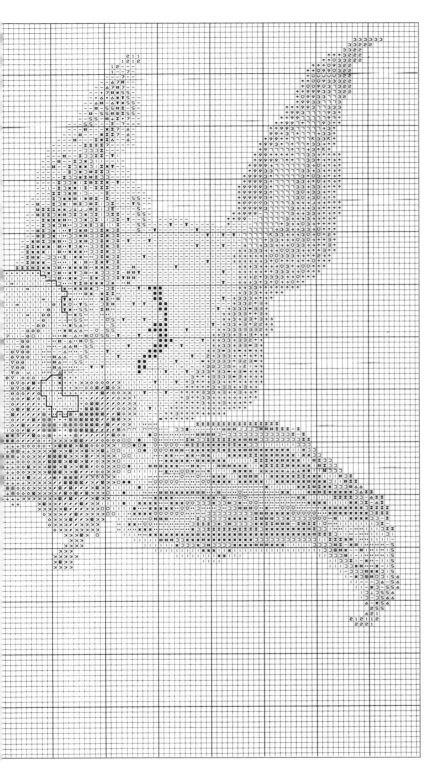

Chart Key

	Anchor	DMC			Anchor	DMC
−	1	blanc	↓		25	963
I	2	712	▽		94	552
1	869	3743	⊖		92	3607
2	225	703	▬		209	913
3	211	986	◉		206	564
5	60	605	∥		238	703
6	85	3609	↖		229	699
7	90	210	→		227	701
9	228	700	↑		226	702
⋈	288	445	⋯		253	472
◇	289	307	▽		254	3348
✦	290	973	⊒		255	907
○	271	819	✳		300	745
⊥	48	818	⊐		301	744
□	23	776	⊒		311	743
⊞	50	894		Backstitch		
			—		1040	647

Mill Hill Beads

●	62042	Purple seed bead
⊞	72009	Lilac bugle bead
▼	02009	Lilac seed bead
■	62034	Dark purple seed bead
⊠	02013	Red seed bead
N	00167	Bright green seed bead
⬍	00525	Pale green seed bead
•|•	00145	Pale pink seed bead
+	02066	Lime green seed bead
⌐	00332	Dark green bead

CROSS STITCH PLUS
RIBBON
EMBROIDERY

Ribbon embroidery is quick and easy and once you have learned the basic stitching techniques, the embroidery will multiply at an astonishing rate, thrilling you with the results. Mixing ribbon work with cross stitch adds a third dimension to a piece, allowing the intricate cross stitches to form a detailed background that is then embellished with beautiful ribbon work.

Ribbons have always been used to adorn fashion garments throughout history. The finer woven ribbons, mainly French, were used in the nineteenth century to copy popular embroidery stitches. By using the soft, pliable ribbon a delicate, three-dimensional embroidery was created. Stitches were chosen and developed to emulate garden flowers and this work was used on small precious items, such as photograph frames and needle cases.

In this chapter we will teach you a variety of ribbon work stitches – from the most basic stab stitch to the more intricate spider-web rose stitch. There are some delightful decorative projects for you to try, introducing the types of stitches gradually so that your confidence grows with the pieces you stitch. In the intermediate project you can practise a few more complicated stitches and in the advanced project we let you loose on a crescendo of floral embroidery. All the stitches are easy to learn, the more advanced ones requiring just a little more tension and needle control to produce a perfect result but this can be achieved with a little practise.

RIBBON EMBROIDERY ▨ BASIC TECHNIQUES

USING THE CHARTS AND THREADING A NEEDLE WITH RIBBON

The instructions for working the ribbon embroidery charts are combined on the cross stitch charts. A coloured line represents a stitch and the key indicates the colour and type of stitch to be used in each position. Follow the comprehensive instructions given here for how to construct each individual stitch and start by threading your needle with ribbon. This particular method is used for threading a needle with ribbon because it is economical and does not allow the ribbon to slip out of the needle when stitching.

1 ▨ Use a short length of ribbon, 12in (30.5cm) at a time to prevent the ribbon from getting damaged and torn. Thread the ribbon through the needle, about 3in (7.5cm).

2 ▨ Take the short end of the ribbon and pierce the needle through 1/2in (1.25cm) from the end of the ribbon. Now take the tip of the needle and gently pull the long end until the ribbon is locked in place.

3 ▨ When all the stitching is finished and the ribbon is safely fastened off, remove the ribbon from the needle by cutting close to the eye of the needle.

STAB STITCH

This is the simplest of all ribbon embroidery stitches.

1 ▨ Thread your needle with ribbon and fasten on by passing it through the back of the cross stitch, then bring the needle up at the position indicated on the chart you are following.

2 ▨ Make the stitch, going back into the fabric at the position indicated on the chart, pulling gently so that a generous stitch is made (see Figure 1). The ribbon should be untwisted and always kept as flat as possible; if it becomes too creased a little stroke with the thumb and forefinger will usually straighten it out.

3 ▨ When all the stitches have been made, fasten off by making a small backstitch through the ribbon on the reverse of the fabric and feed the ribbon through the back of the cross stitch.

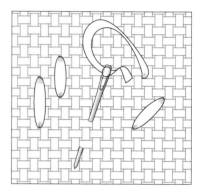

FIGURE 1

INVERTED STAB STITCH

This is a slightly more complicated variation of stab stitch.

1 ▨ Fasten on (see step 1 of stab stitch). The ribbon should be untwisted and always kept as flat as possible. If it becomes too creased, stroke it with the thumb and forefinger.

2 ▨ Hold the ribbon gently over the position where you wish the stitch to finish (as indicated on the chart you are following), then pierce the ribbon with the needle, stitching *into* the ribbon (see Figure 2).

3 ▨ Pull gently on the ribbon until a neat end is formed. If you pull too hard the stitch will become thin and you will lose the inverted end. When all the stitches have been made, fasten off (see step 3 of stab stitch).

FIGURE 2

MOCK BULLION STITCH

This stitch produces a rich look and three-dimensional quality to your embroidery.

1 ⊠ Thread your needle with ribbon and fasten on by passing it through the back of the cross stitch, then bring the needle up at the position indicated on the chart you are following and make a stab stitch.

2 ⊠ Bring your needle up at the end of the stab stitch, ensuring that your ribbon is flat and untwisted (figure 3a), then, using the eye of the needle, wrap the

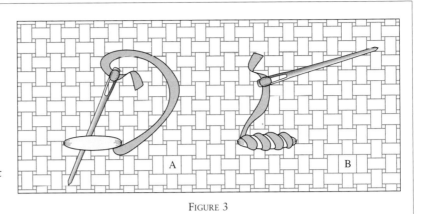

FIGURE 3

ribbon gently around the stab stitch making sure that it lies flat. Untwist the ribbon and repeat the wrapping four or five times until a neat mock bullion is formed (see Figure 3b).

3 ⊠ When all the stitches have been made, fasten off by making a small backstitch through the ribbon on the reverse of the fabric and then feed the ribbon through the back of the cross stitch.

SPIDER-WEB ROSE STITCH

This lovely stitch looks complicated but is in fact quite easy to achieve, looking like a pretty flower on completion.

1 ⊠ Using four strands of stranded cotton and a size 24 tapestry needle, fasten on through the back of the cross stitch and bring the needle up at one of the positions indicated on the chart you are following.

2 ⊠ Make five straight stitches (spokes) into the central hole as shown in Figure 4a, then fasten off the stranded cotton by passing it through the back of the cross stitch.

3 ⊠ Thread a needle with ribbon and fasten on by passing it through the back of the cross stitch. Bring the needle up near the centre of the spokes and thread the ribbon round in a circle, threading over and

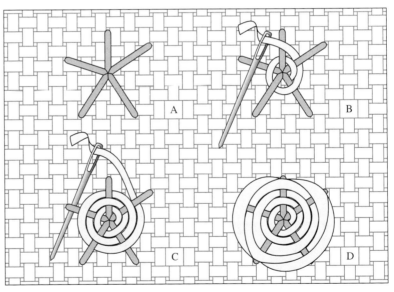

FIGURE 4

under each spoke in succession (see Figure 4b). Continue threading in and out of the spokes making sure that the ribbon is not twisted and lays flat. As you get nearer to the outside of the 'roses' the stitches will get longer and more generous (see Figures 4c and 4d).

4 ⊠ Once all the room on the spokes has been filled, fasten off by making a small backstitch through the ribbon on the reverse of the fabric and feed the ribbon through the back of the cross stitch.

IRIS STITCH

This deceptively simple stitch, once again intended to mimic a flower shape, requires a little more needle control but is very effective.

1 ◼ Thread your needle with ribbon and fasten on by passing it through the cross stitch, then bring the needle up at the position indicated on the chart you are following.

2 ◼ Bring the needle out through the fabric at the point marked with an arrow on Figure 6a. Stitch loops, varying the lengths to produce different size 'flowers', anchoring the top of each loop with a small stitch. The bottom of the loop will then form the middle of the iris stitch.

3 ◼ To form the outside petals, bring the needle up through the fabric as indicated by the arrow on Figure 6b. Turn the needle round and, using the blunt end (to avoid catching the ribbon with the sharp end), drag the needle under the bottom of the loops. There is no need to stitch any fabric in this move. Now push the needle back through the fabric so the two outside petals match lengths. This is the iris.

4 ◼ Take two strands of lemon stranded cotton and stitch a French knot (see page 9) into the centre of the chain loop. If you want you could add more French knots to each flower.

5 ◼ When all the stitches have been made, fasten off by making a small backstitch on the reverse of the fabric and feed the ribbon through the back of the cross stitch.

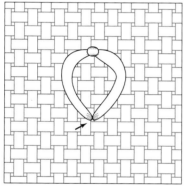

FIGURE 6A

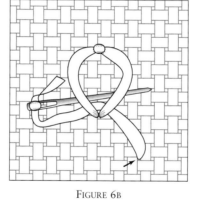

FIGURE 6B

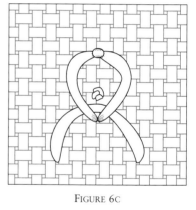

FIGURE 6C

RIBBON FRENCH KNOT

This is a ribbon work equivalent of a French knot (see page 9) and produces a neat mound, ideal for accenting parts of a piece.

1 ◼ Thread your needle with ribbon and fasten on by passing it through the cross stitch, then bring the needle up at the position indicated on the chart you are following. Put the needle under the ribbon and twist the ribbon once around the needle.

2 ◼ Put the needle back into the fabric, near the spot you brought it out. Pull the thread gently. This will form the shape of your knot around the needle. Pull the needle through the fabric very slowly, retaining the already formed knot shape, until all the thread is through. Take care, if you pull too harshly or put the needle back into the same spot, the knot will disappear through the fabric. If you don't handle the ribbon firmly you will get a floppy knot but if you pull too tightly you will not be able to pull the needle through.

3 ◼ When all stitches have been made, fasten off with a small backstitch on the back of the fabric and feed the ribbon through the back of the cross stitch.

LOOPED PETAL DAISY STITCH

Another stitch that was designed to mimic a flower, this daisy stitch is sure to create a fresh look to any ribbon embroidery.

1 ▣ Thread your needle with ribbon and fasten on by passing it through the back of the cross stitch, then bring the needle up at the position indicated on the chart you are following. Take the ribbon up through the fabric, at a corner junction of a cross stitch (see Figure 5a). Try to keep the ribbon as flat as possible.

2 ▣ Put the needle down through the fabric, behind the ribbon, as shown by the arrow in Figure 5a. Pull very gently to control the ribbon, until the petal is formed to your liking (every petal you stitch will be slightly different so don't panic). Now you can either anchor every petal with a pin as

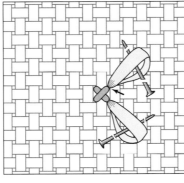

FIGURE 5A

FIGURE 5B

shown or take a risk and hold it with your thumb and finger (at worse you'll lose your petal through the fabric and have to start again).

3 ▣ Stitch a petal for each corner of the cross stitch (see Figure 5b). You will have to force the needle through to make the fifth petal – this can be anywhere you choose.

4 ▣ Anchor all the petals at their bases with an individual French

knot using stranded cotton (see page 9) and arrange the rest to form a clump in the centre. If you have used the pin method, you can now remove them.

5 ▣ When all the stitches have been made, fasten off by making a small backstitch through the ribbon on the reverse of the fabric and feed the ribbon through the back of the cross stitch.

RIBBON EMBROIDERY ▣ TOOLS OF THE TRADE

FABRIC

Any fabric suitable for cross stitch can be used for ribbon work but it may be necessary to change the width of the ribbon depending on the count of the fabric you are using.

RIBBON

The ribbons used in this chapter are much lighter than the normal satin haberdashery ribbons. We would advise you not to embroider with these as they are too thick to control easily.

Silk ribbon Pure silk ribbon is available in different widths, however, with our cross stitch we have use a 3.5mm width. It is beautifully soft as it is made from 100% silk and can be easily pulled through the fabric. Although silk ribbon is colour-fast we do not recommend you wash it as the stitches are very delicate and can get squashed.

Rayon ribbon The other type of ribbon that is widely used is made from rayon, an artificial fibre. We have used the 4mm width from Offray. It is slightly crisper and can be laundered, which can be useful.

~ AFGHAN BLANKET, MITTENS AND HAT ~

SMALL STARTS

To introduce the technique of ribbon embroidery we have chosen this beautiful baby's blanket, an afghan, with matching mittens and hat. The first stitches that you will learn are some of the most basic in ribbon work – stab stitch and looped petal daisy stitch. Although the idea of stitching with ribbon may seem a little daunting at first, with a little practise you will find that the work grows very quickly and is extremely simple to complete.

MATERIALS

Cream Afghan Anne (6 x 8 pattern squares) for the blanket

Cream Afghan Anne (1 square each) for the mittens and hat

Stranded cottons as listed in the key

Tapestry needles size 22 and 24

Crewel needle size 7

Silk or Offray ribbon as listed in the key

A hat and pair of mittens of your choice

This enchanting baby's blanket with matching mittens and hat, is covered with kittens, mice and heart motifs. The colour scheme is bright and contemporary, but if you would prefer to stitch it in traditional pastel colours these could easily be swapped for the colour palette of the heart motifs. The blanket could easily be stitched using only one of the animal designs featured, you could then replace the other one with a motif of your choice.

WORKING THE MITTENS AND HAT EMBROIDERY

1 ⊠ Mount your afghan square in a hoop or frame and, following the charts on page 40, use a waste knot to start (see Cross Stitch Basic Techniques page 11). Work the animal designs – these are stitched with four strands of stranded cotton over two fabric threads using a size 24 tapestry needle.

2 ⊠ When all the cross stitch is complete, stitch the ribbon looped petal daisy stitches on the kittens and the stab stitch sail boats on the mice. There is a central gap left on the chart to show you the position for the single looped petal daisy stitch on each kitten. The yellow lines on the mouse chart represent the length of the stab stitches to be made to represent the sails.

3 ⊠ Once all the stitching is complete, wash the piece gently and press lightly into a thick, fluffy towel.

4 ⊠ Fray the top, bottom and sides of the square by removing the threads up to the thicker line of weave and hand stitch or machine a line of zigzag stitches to hold the rest of the threads in place.

5 ⊠ To finish, position and pin the squares into place on the hat and mittens. Stitch the motifs onto the hat and mittens with a slipstitch using one strand of stranded cotton and a crewel needle size 7.

WORKING THE BLANKET EMBROIDERY

1 ⊠ Mount your afghan fabric in a hoop or frame and, following the charts on pages 38–39, use a waste knot to start (see Cross Stitch Basic Techniques page 11). Begin the cross

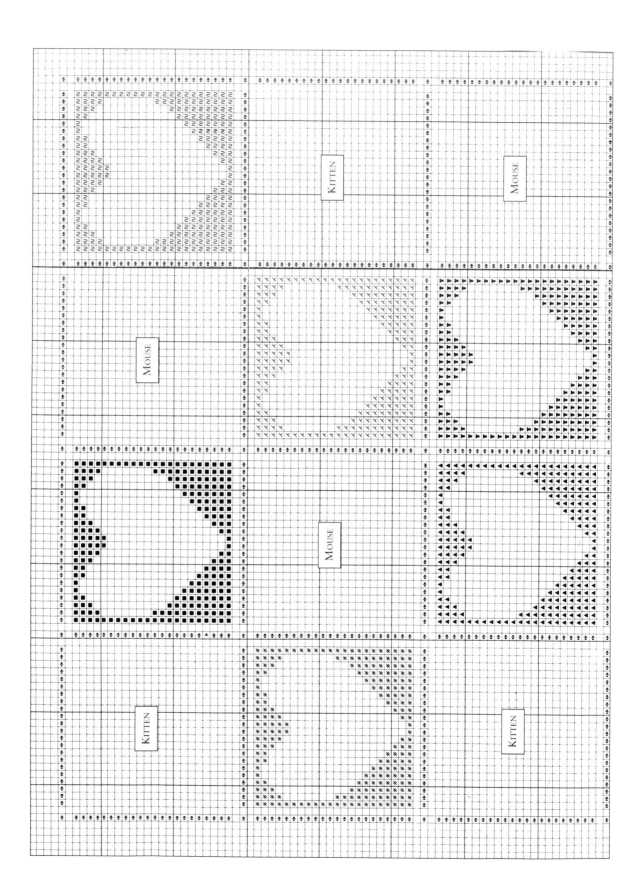

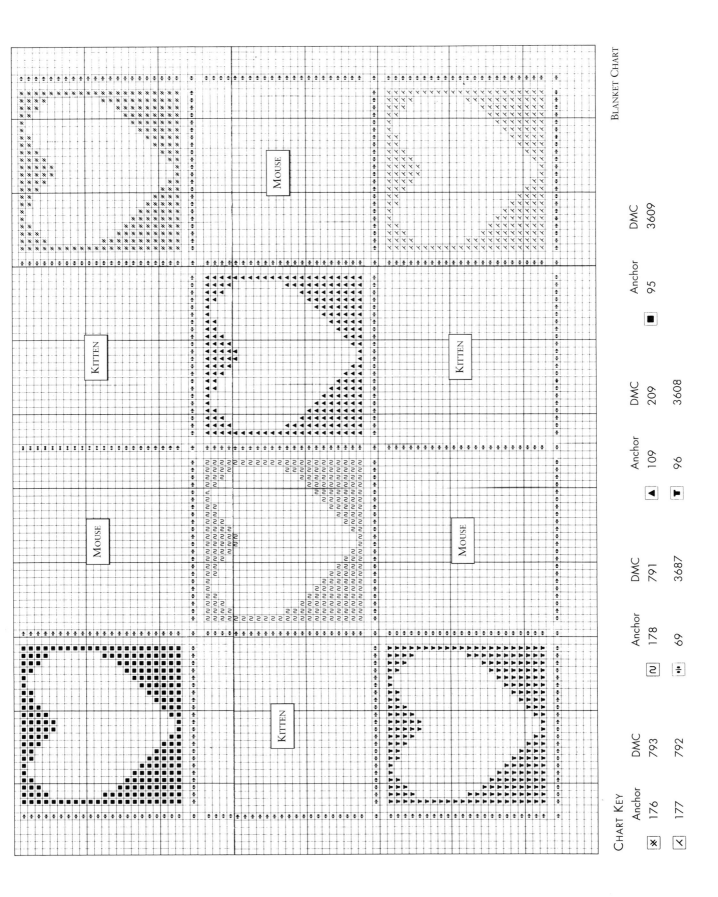

BLANKET CHART

MOUSE

KITTEN

KITTEN

MOUSE

MOUSE

KITTEN

CHART KEY							
Anchor	DMC	Anchor	DMC	Anchor	DMC	Anchor	DMC
176	793	178	791	109	209	95	3609
177	792	69	3687	96	3608		

Kitten Chart Key

	Anchor	DMC
◨	176	793
Y	177	792
··	381	938
▽	375	869
✱	373	437
T	96	3608
■	95	3609

Backstitch
— 403 310

French Knots
 290 973

Ribbon
 Silk (3.5mm) Offray (4mm)
Looped petal daisy stitch
 12 617

Mouse Chart Key

	Anchor	DMC
ꞁ	905	3781
⬉	235	414
◸	398	415
◩	176	793
Y	177	792
·ꞁ·	69	3687
··	381	938

Backstitch
— 403 310

Ribbon
 Silk (3.5mm) Offray (4mm)
Stab stitch
� 3 028

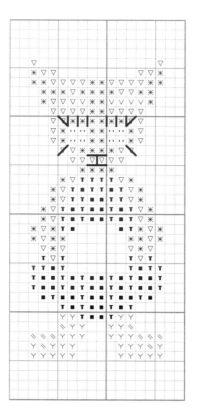

KITTEN CHART

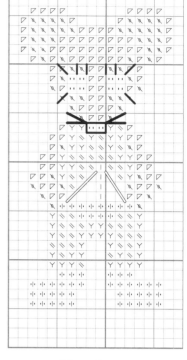

MOUSE CHART

stitch at the first heart motif at the top of the blanket, leaving half a square all round for fraying. Work the cross stitch for the heart motifs and the border in six strands of stranded cotton, over four fabric threads using a size 22 tapestry needle. Separate and recombine your cotton before stitching, see Cross Stitch Basic Techniques page 10. The heart motifs fit in the fabric squares with one fabric thread spare all round. Count the threads to ensure the central positioning of the first design and follow this placement for the rest of the heart motifs.

2 ⊠ Once all the heart motifs and the square border have been stitched, you can begin to stitch the animal designs. These are worked in four strands of stranded cotton over two fabric threads using a size 24 tapestry needle.

3 ⊠ Next work the backstitch in two strands of stranded cotton. Stitch the ribbon daisies stitches on the kittens and the stab stitch sail boats on the mice. There is a central gap left on the chart to show the position for the single looped petal daisy stitch on each kitten. Work French knots in the centre of the daisy in four strands of stranded cotton. The yellow lines on the mouse chart represent the length of the stab stitches to be made to represent the sails.

4 ⊠ Wash and press the piece gently. Fray the top, bottom and sides of the blanket by removing the threads up to the thicker line of weave and then hand stitch or machine a line of zigzag stitches to hold the rest of the threads securely in place.

~ BAY TREE GLASSES CASE ~

FLOWERING

RIBBON SKILLS

The two projects in this section, the sewing bag and matching glasses case, combine cross stitch and ribbon embroidery to create a lovely spring look. Both are easy to stitch, allowing you to add further ribbon work stitches to your repertoire. Remember ribbon work is a free-style embroidery so each piece of work will be unique.

MATERIALS

14 count Zweigart Aida in cream, 9 x 12in (23 x 30.5cm) or to fit your glasses

Stranded cottons as listed in the key

Offray or silk ribbon as listed in the key

Tapestry needle size 24

Crewel needle size 7

Small piece of backing fabric of your choice

Two small pieces of wadding

Two small pieces of felt

Length of cord for decoration

This glasses case is ideal for trying the perfect combination of ribbon work and cross stitch. The looped petal daisy stitches really add to the three-dimensional quality of the embroidery. This case is perfect for any size of glasses and is stitched with synthetic ribbon, however you could substitute silk ribbon to create a really special present.

WORKING THE EMBROIDERY

1 ⊠ Mount the Aida in a hoop or frame and, following the chart on page 44, use a waste knot to start (see Cross Stitch Basic Techniques page 11). Begin with the cross stitch, using two strands of stranded cotton and a tapestry needle size 24. You may find it easier to start at the bottom of the main plant pot rather than in the middle of the spindly tree trunk, if so make sure that you have enough fabric for the design.

2 ⊠ When the cross stitch is complete, wash and press your piece and try to keep it clean when working the ribbon embroidery as it will not be washed again, especially if silk ribbon is used.

3 ⊠ Following the chart, start the ribbon work. The coloured crosses marked on the chart will show you the placement of each stitch and the key will show you the stitch and type of ribbon to use. Refer to Ribbon Work Techniques on page 32 to help you with the looped petal daisy stitch.

4 ⊠ If you wish to add a bow at the base of the tree, simply tie a bow of the correct size and attach it with

two strands of stranded cotton with French knots at intervals.

MAKING UP THE GLASSES CASE

1 ⊠ First make the pattern for the case. Draw a rectangle a little larger than your glasses. Cut this out in paper and fold it in half lengthways, rounding off the bottom end (you could use the base of a mug for this). Allow ½in (1.25cm) for seam allowance. Check at this stage it is big enough for your own glasses.

2 ⊠ Cut out your embroidered piece to the same size as the pattern, checking that the tree is central. Cut out one piece of backing fabric, two pieces of felt and two pieces of wadding, all the same size as the pattern.

3 ⊠ Put the right sides of the backing fabric and the embroidered piece together. Pin, tack and stitch on the stitching line which is ½in (1.25cm) from the edge, leaving the top edge open. Clip the seam close to the stitching, remove the pins and tacking, then turn through.

4 ⊠ Repeat the above step with the pieces of felt and wadding together. Fit the felt case inside the embroidered one. Turn the top inside neatly and slipstitch all the way round the top.

5 ⊠ We added a decorative cord by hand stitching as this not only looks pretty but also prevents wearing of the edges. Tie knots to finish off the cord. Add a button or press-stud to fasten.

41

~ BAY TREE SEWING BAG ~

MATERIALS

27 count Zweigart
Meran fabric in lemon (237),
18 x 14in (46 x 35.5cm)

Stranded cottons as
listed in the key

Silk or Offray ribbon
as listed in the key

Tapestry needle size 24

Crewel needle size 7

Firm cotton lining fabric
of your choice, 16in (40cm) x
full width of fabric

Sewing thread to match
the fabric of your choice

Piece of felt, 15in (38cm) square

Piece of calico (or other firm
cotton), 24 x 12in (61 x 30.5cm)

Piece of wadding, 24 x 12in
(61 x 30.5cm)

Length of satin ribbon of your
choice for fastening

Two buttons of your choice

Two small pieces of Velcro or
press-studs for pockets

This sewing bag provides a way to enjoy embroidery and make a useful object. Cross stitch and ribbon work combine to create a spring feel in this bay tree design. The sewing bag is large enough to hold a 6in (15cm) hoop, and many other items. It is worked in silk ribbon but you could use synthetic ribbon.

WORKING THE EMBROIDERY

1 ⊠ Mount the fabric in a hoop or frame and, following the chart on page 45, use a waste knot to start (see Starting Work page 11). Begin with the cross stitch, using two strands of stranded cotton over two threads and a tapestry needle size 24. You may find it easier to start at the bottom of the main plant pot rather than in the middle of the spindly tree trunk, if so make sure that you have enough fabric for the design.

2 ⊠ When you have completed the cross stitch wash and press your piece now and try to keep it clean when working the ribbon embroidery as it will not be washed again if silk ribbon is used.

3 ⊠ Following the chart, start the ribbon work. The coloured crosses marked on the chart will show you the placement of each stitch and the key will show you the stitch and type of ribbon to use. Refer to Ribbon Work Techniques on page 32 to help you with the looped petal daisy stitch and iris stitch. Use ribbon French knots for the forget-me-nots – stitch these with ribbon first and then fill the centres with lemon stranded cotton, using two strands and a size 7 crewel needle.

MAKING UP THE BAG

First make the pockets and the hoop holder, altering these to suit your own needs.

1 ⊠ To make the pockets, cut two pieces of felt 5½ x 10in (14 x 25.5cm). Cut two pieces of lining fabric of your choice, 7 x 13in (18 x 33cm).

2 ⊠ Place the piece of felt on to the wrong side of the fabric. Fold the sides and bottom over the felt by ½in (1.25cm) and press. Take the top edge and fold the fabric under twice to make a neat edge, then stitch the top edge. Make another pocket in the same way.

3 ⊠ For the hoop holder cut two pieces of felt 1½ x 7in (4 x 18cm). Cut one piece of fabric of your choice 3 x 8½in (7.5 x 21.5cm).

4 ⊠ Press all the edges of the fabric over the felt in the same way as you did for the pockets. Put the other piece of felt over the top to cover all the raw edges, then topstitch to form a neat band. You could use your initials as part of the top stitching or try a decorative stitch on the machine.

5 ⊠ Cut a piece of lining fabric, a piece of wadding and a piece of firm cotton (such as calico), all to measure 22 x 10in (56 x 25.5cm). Make a sandwich with the fabric on top, then the wadding and finally the calico. Pin and tack these layers together to form a firm base.

6 ▣ Pin, tack and then stitch the pockets in place though all three layers. Use a press-stud, Velcro or other way of closing the pockets.

7 ▣ Pin, tack and stitch the hoop attachment on one edge, in the centre of the three sections. Use two buttons with buttonholes to fasten.

8 ▣ Now cut your embroidered piece to 8 x 10in (20 x 25.5cm), making sure your embroidery is central. If you wish at this stage you can add a ribbon stitched border, as we have done. This is a border of running stitches using silk ribbon and a French knot to anchor the running stitches in the centre. The running stitch was worked over ten threads about 1½in (4cm) from the cut edge.

9 ▣ Now cut a piece of lining fabric 10 x 14in (25.5 x 35.5cm). Seam the fabric to your embroidery matching right sides together. Stitch ½in (1.25cm) down the left-hand side edge of the bay tree, then press the seam. For more stability add iron-on interfacing to the wrong side.

10 ▣ Place the two finished pieces right sides together. Pin, tack, then stitch around carefully leaving enough space at the bottom edge to turn the work through. Clip and trim the edges as this will make it easier to turn. Remove the pins and tacking, turn the work through and slipstitch the gap closed.

11 ▣ Finally topstitch into three sections – this will help the bag to fold easily when you are using it. Add a fastening of your choice – we used a length of ribbon.

BAY TREE GLASSES CASE CHART

CHART KEY

	Anchor	DMC		Anchor	DMC	
◹	369	434	÷	210	562	
╱	374	420	+	218	561	
╲	883	3064	♡	358	801	
◰	368	437	RIBBONS		Silk	Offray
∧	906	829	═ Looped daisy petals			
					3	28
Y	209	913	Blue bow		132	316

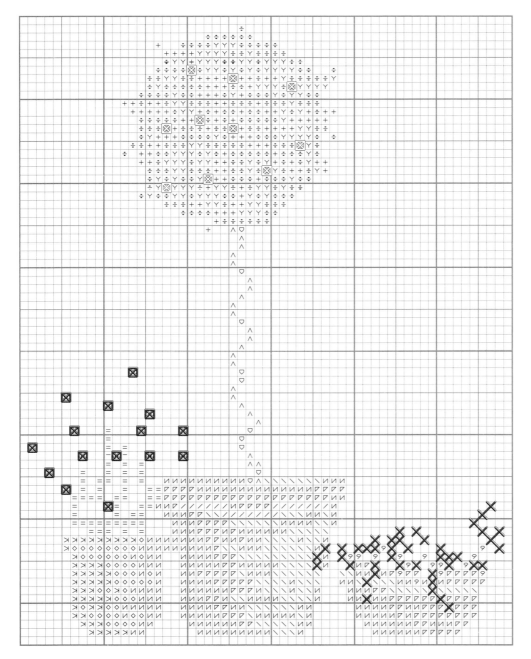

BAY TREE SEWING BAG CHART

CHART KEY

	Anchor	DMC			Anchor	DMC
9	258	904		◥	883	3064
=	244	701		И	368	437
⊁	881	945		∧	906	829
◇	362	738		Y	209	913
◿	369	434		÷	210	562
∕	374	420		+	218	561
				▽	358	801

RIBBONS		Silk	Offray
═══	Looped daisy petals		
		3	28
━━	French		
	knot (mixed)	44	345
		10	303
━━━	Iris (mixed)	22	463
		118	467

~ GARDEN STATUE PICTURE ~

GROWING AND
SHOWING

Your skills will grow further in this advanced ribbon work design. We have combined all the stitches that you have learnt so far with some more complicated ones – spider-web roses and mock bullion stitches – allowing you really to show off. Although the method of completing these stitches is no more difficult than any other ribbon work stitch, they do require slightly more control to achieve a truly magnificent result.

MATERIALS
28 count Zweigart Linen in light blue, 17 x 23in (35.5 x 58.5cm)

Stranded cottons as listed in the key

Silk ribbon as listed in the key, no Offray alternative has been offered as close equivalents for many of the colours cannot be matched

Tapestry needle size 24

Crewel needle size 7

Frame of your choice

This design features a stone statue surrounded by a beautiful rose arch in full bloom. The garden in which the statue stands is blooming in all its summer glory with irises, ox-eye daisies, forget-me-not, snapdragons, American poppies and delphiniums. The cross stitch is worked first and provides an excellent background for the delicate ribbon embroidery.

WORKING THE EMBROIDERY
1 ⊠ Mount the fabric in a hoop or frame and, following the chart on pages 48–49, use a waste knot to start (see Cross Stitch Basic Techniques page 11) in the centre of the fabric. Begin the cross stitch with two strands of stranded cotton over two fabric threads using a size 24 tapestry needle. Work the backstitch in one strand.

2 ⊠ Once all the cross stitch is complete, wash and press the embroidery into a thick, fluffy towel.

3 ⊠ Start the ribbon embroidery, following the chart and key (see Ribbon Embroidery Techniques page 32 for the stitches). When the stitching is completed we do not recommend that you wash the piece as the ribbon stitches may be damaged.

4 ⊠ Mount the embroidery in a frame of your choice (see Finishing Techniques page 126)

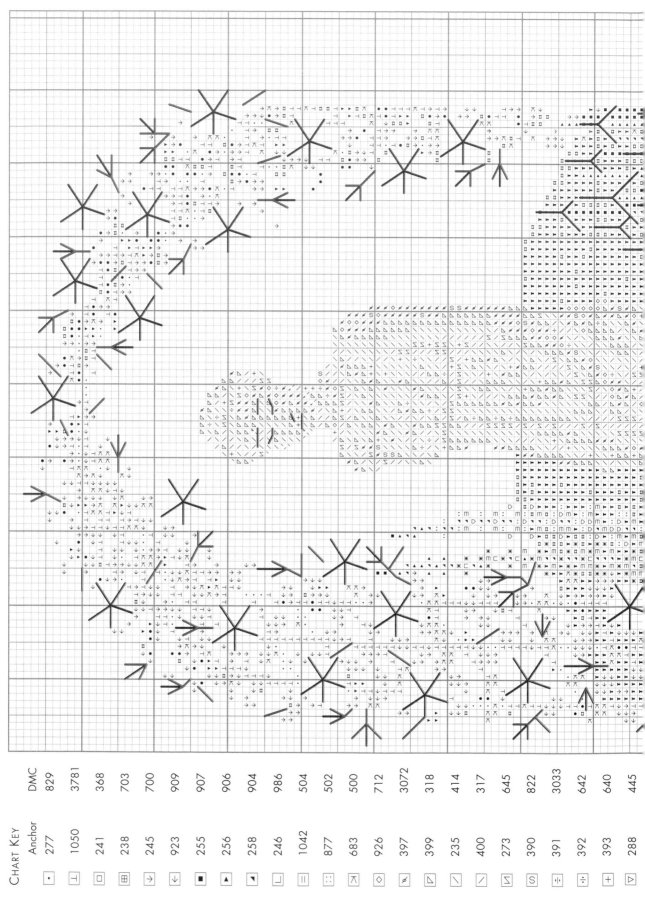

CHART KEY																							
DMC	829	3781	368	703	700	909	907	906	904	986	504	502	500	712	3072	318	414	317	645	822	3033	642	640	445
Anchor	277	1050	241	238	245	923	255	256	258	246	1042	877	683	926	397	399	235	400	273	390	391	392	393	288
	⊡	⊤	□	⊞	→	↓	■	▲	◥	⌐	‖	∷	⊼	◇	⌀	◺	\	/	⊿	S	⊶	÷	+	▷

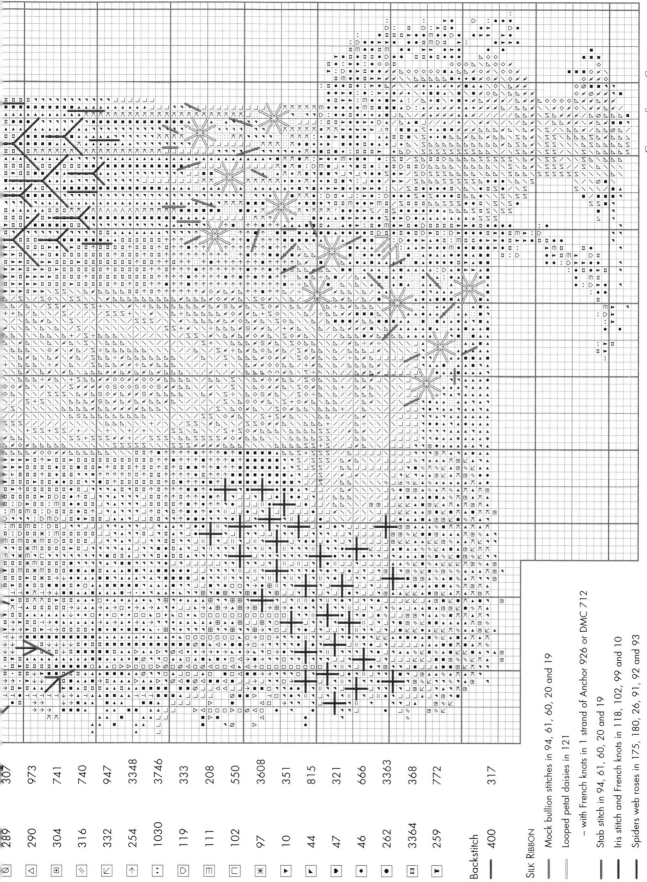

GARDEN STATUE CHART

⊘	289	307
◁	290	973
◉	304	741
◊	316	740
◣	332	947
↑	254	3348
⁙	1030	3746
◨	119	333
▥	111	208
▭	102	550
✳	97	3608
▶	10	351
◤	44	815
▸	47	321
◆	46	666
●	262	3363
▣	3364	368
▸	259	772

Backstitch

—— 400   317

SILK RIBBON

	Mock bullion stitches in 94, 61, 60, 20 and 19
	Looped petal daisies in 121
	– with French knots in 1 strand of Anchor 926 or DMC 712
	Stab stitch in 94, 61, 60, 20 and 19
	Iris stitch and French knots in 118, 102, 99 and 10
	Spiders web roses in 175, 180, 26, 91, 92 and 93

CROSS STITCH PLUS
COUNTED
SATIN STITCH

Counted satin stitch is a deceptively simple embroidery technique which produces quite wonderful results. As with all counted thread work, it is achieved by the counting of fabric threads and the careful placement of the stitches. Counted satin stitch consists of blocks of straight stitches placed together in patterns, borders and spot motifs to form a whole design. This chapter shows how attractive and versatile the stitch can be, but more particularly shows how effective it is when combined with cross stitch.

By turning the direction of satin stitches, the sheen and lustre of the thread is shown to best advantage, revealing the reason behind the name 'satin' stitch, particularly when silk threads are used. The whole atmosphere of satin stitch embroidery can be further altered by using varied threads, such as sophisticated metallic or space-dyed threads.

Satin stitch has been used for hundreds of years in Japanese embroidery, particularly on their delicate kimonos. To qualify as a professional embroiderer in Japan requires a seven year apprenticeship but you'll be glad to know that the satin stitch in this chapter won't take that amount of time to perfect, in fact it is a natural progression from cross stitch and grows much more quickly.

The exciting contemporary projects are easy to make, beginning with two simple paperweights and we're sure they will get you hooked on this type of embroidery. The threads used in this chapter are just as exciting, particularly the space-dyed threads and the metallic blending filament. With the medium-sized projects we have adapted a traditional alphabet sampler to this new technique with stunning results. The advanced project, a magnificent footstool alive with wildlife, then allows you to practise and expand your new skills on a grand scale.

COUNTED SATIN STITCH ◼ BASIC TECHNIQUES

PREPARING AND USING THREAD

In this chapter we have used a variety of threads for stitching the cross stitch and counted satin stitch, some of these threads using more than one strand. The lay and direction of the thread is important in counted satin stitch, so just a little extra time spent in thread preparation is definitely worthwhile.

STITCHING WITH MULTIPLE STRANDS

Preparing thread properly is worth the effort as the thread will cover the fabric better and more evenly, giving the work a neater, smoother appearance.

1 ◼ Take a length of thread about 20in (50cm) long and separate out all the individual strands. With stranded cotton this means separating out the six strands.

2 ◼ Holding each separate thread at the top, allow each to unwind a little, so that when they are recombined they do not tangle.

3 ◼ Recombine the threads, again holding them at the top and stroking along the length to flatten the strands out.

4 ◼ Thread the needle carefully so that the strands are flat and even.

STITCHING WITH METALLIC THREAD

Metallic thread creates some lovely effects but can be a little awkward to work with. You will probably find it easier to work with quite short lengths of thread to avoid tangling.

STITCHING WITH SPACE-DYED THREAD

Caron Watercolours thread, which is a three-ply thread, has been used in this chapter. We have used the thread in single strands, though two could be used if coverage is insufficient with one. To prepare the space-dyed thread for stitching first undo the skein and cut the bottom of the loop so that it is now in lengths. Re-thread these lengths back through the name tag to keep them tidy. We recommend stitching with a half length as this keeps the thread from becoming fuzzy.

STITCHING ON DIFFERENT FABRICS

Any fabric suitable for cross stitch is also suitable for counted satin stitch. For further advice, see Materials and Equipment page 6.

Aida With Aida fabric the threads are woven in blocks and the stitches are made by taking the thread over the fabric blocks, as you can see in Figure 1 below.

Evenweave In evenweave fabrics the threads are woven singly, and the stitches are made by taking the thread you are stitching with over each of the fabric threads (see Figure 2).

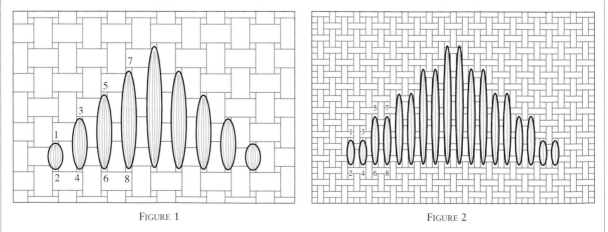

FIGURE 1   FIGURE 2

STITCHING SATIN STITCH

For such a simple stitch, satin stitch is extremely versatile and many wonderful designs can be created with it, especially when combined with cross stitch.

1 ⊠ If using more than one strand of cotton or thread, prepare it for stitching as described above and then start with a waste knot with a long thread (see Cross Stitch Basic Techniques page 11).

2 ⊠ Bring the needle up at the position indicated on the chart. Trying to keep the threads as flat as possible, put the needle back into the fabric at the point indicated on the chart. Follow the numbers on the chart for the order of stitching.

3 ⊠ At this point some people prefer to use a laying tool to keep the strands flat. This is done by lifting and stroking the stitch as

the needle is threaded back into the fabric. Once complete, the stitch is stroked again to ensure alignment of the threads.

4 ⊠ Continue stitching until all the satin stitches are complete. Fasten off by taking the thread through the back of a few stitches and securing with a small backstitch. Cut off the waste knot and fasten off the 'tail' in the same way.

USING THE CHARTS

Some of the charts for counted satin stitch are combined charts, where a group of symbols represent an area of satin stitch to be worked. The direction of the stitching is indicated either in the text or on the chart itself. For the Brown Bear Footstool there is a separate chart for the satin stitch (page 68). In this chart each line

of the grid represents a single fabric thread and the key indicates the colour and number of strands to be used.

⊠ The first type of chart uses traditional cross stitch symbols to show the placing of the satin stitches (see Figure 3 below left). We show you how this would translate on to Aida in satin stitch

(see Figure 4). The stitches are numbered to illustrate the order of stitching.

⊠ The second type of chart indicates the precise placement and direction of stitching on evenweave fabric, where each line represents one fabric thread (see Figure 5).

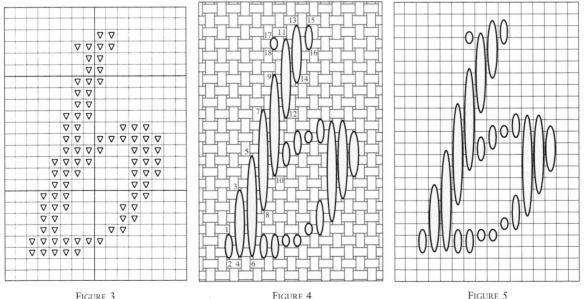

FIGURE 3   FIGURE 4   FIGURE 5

COUNTED SATIN STITCH ◼ TOOLS OF THE TRADE

FABRIC

Any fabric which can be used for cross stitch may also be used for counted satin stitch, making the various types of Aida and evenweave perfect. The important feature of the fabric is that it is made up of threads that can be counted easily, where there are the same number of warp and weft threads to the inch (2.5cm). Some of the projects in this chapter use Aida Plus, a newly developed fabric. This has all the benefits of regular Aida plus some of the advantages of plastic canvas, in that it can be stitched without an embroidery frame and cut and shaped without fraying.

HIGHLIGHTER PEN

You may already use one of these for your cross stitch work and they are particularly helpful in counted satin stitch, allowing you to mark on the chart which stitches have been completed.

LAYING TOOL

This is a long, thin tool traditionally used when embroidering satin stitch. The tip of the tool is used to stroke the stitches into place individually to ensure that they are lying correctly and maximizes the shine on the threads.

THREADS

The following four threads have been used in this chapter.

Stranded cotton Stranded cotton thread is a six-ply mercerised cotton and is available in a vast colour range. The cotton is very silky by nature and as such is perfect for satin stitch, giving the smooth finish required in some of the designs.

Shaded threads Shaded threads or space-dyed threads are coloured by a special process where the dye is dripped on at different intervals and in different colours. The dyes are left to bleed into the threads giving the most unique effects. Because of the process no two threads are exactly the same. The Caron Watercolours range of threads is magnificent, with some names sounding almost edible such as Burnt Toast, Vanilla, and Marigold.

Metallic thread Metallic threads are an exciting modern development, consisting of pieces of metal wrapped around or woven into the thread so they may be stitched easily. There are various ranges on the market, available in different colours and weights. For the Little Princess Cushion (page 60) we have used Kreinik threads, combining the stranded cotton with a blending filament to give an added sparkle to your cross stitch.

Pearl cotton Pearl cotton (or cotton perlé) is 100% cotton and unlike the usual stranded cotton it is not a multi-ply thread but a highly twisted single-ply, producing the effect of shine and shadow particularly when stitched in blocks.

~ PICTURE PAPERWEIGHTS ~

SMALL BUT SMART

*The bright, modern designs
of these three desk-top projects
are sure to cheer up any study.
Combined with cross stitch,
the satin stitch in the
paperweights and notepaper
block is simple and the patterns
allow you to get to grips with
the basic techniques while
creating useful items.*

MATERIALS
FOR THE SMALL SQUARE PAPERWEIGHT
*14 count Aida Plus in white,
5in (12.5cm) square*

Stranded cottons as listed in the key

Tapestry needles size 24 and 22

*Glass paperweight, 2in (5cm) square
(see Suppliers page 127)*

FOR THE DOUBLE FRAME
PAPERWEIGHT
*14 count Aida Plus in white,
5 x 7in (12.5 x 17.5cm)*

Stranded cottons as listed in the key

Tapestry needles size 24 and 22

*Glass paperweight, 2 x 3¹/₂in
(5 x 9cm) (see Suppliers page 127)*

*These two delightful paperweights
can display pictures of your
choice. The colours of the square
paperweight – bold blue combined
with gentle pastel shades – mirror
sunlight reflecting off a watery
pool. The double paperweight
colours were inspired by a crashing
arctic ocean. The instructions are
the same for both paperweights.*

WORKING THE EMBROIDERY
1 ⊠ Start in the centre, using a
waste knot with a long thread (see
Cross Stitch Basic Techniques page
11). Following the charts on page
56, work the cross stitch in two
strands of stranded cotton and a
size 24 tapestry needle.

2 ⊠ Once all the cross stitch is
complete, work the satin stitch
from the chart, using six strands
of stranded cotton and a size 22
tapestry needle. The placement of
the stitches is indicated on the chart
on page 58 by the symbols enclosed
within the black lines. The arrows
indicate the direction of the satin
stitching.

3 ⊠ When all the embroidery is
finished, cut off any waste knots,
threading any 'tails' onto a needle
and passing the thread through the
back of a few stitches. Now
dampen the embroidery slightly
and press right side down into a
thick, fluffy towel to avoid
flattening the stitches.

4 ⊠ Take the paperweight and
place it over the embroidery
centrally. With a pair of sharp
scissors trim the embroidery to size,
then trim the inner aperture
carefully, close to the stitches. Place
your selected photograph(s) or
picture(s) under the frame and then
mount them in the paperweight
according to the manufacturer's
instructions.

DOUBLE FRAME PAPERWEIGHT CHART

CHART KEY

	Anchor	DMC
⊞	177	792
◹	120	3747
◇	175	794
=	1037	3756
∾	178	791

SMALL SQUARE PAPERWEIGHT CHART

~ NOTEPAPER BLOCK ~

MATERIALS
14 count Aida Plus in white,
12¹/₂ x 6¹/₂in (32 x 16.5cm)

Stranded cottons as
listed in the key

Tapestry needles size 24 and 22

Notepaper block,
4 x 3¹/₂in (10 x 9cm)
(see Suppliers page 127)

You can fill the frames in this notepaper block with any picture to make it truly personal.

WORKING THE EMBROIDERY

1 ⊠ Start in the centre, using a waste knot with a long thread (see Cross Stitch Basic Techniques page 11). Following the chart on page 58, work all the cross stitch in two strands of stranded cotton and a size 24 tapestry needle. Note that only one section of the chart is shown.

2 ⊠ Next work the satin stitch using six strands of stranded cotton and a size 22 tapestry needle. The placement of the stitches is indicated on the chart by the symbols

enclosed within the black outlined diamonds. The arrows indicate the direction of the stitching.

3 ⊠ When all the embroidery is finished, cut off any waste knots, threading any 'tails' through the back of a few stitches. Dampen the embroidery and press right side down into a soft towel.

4 ⊠ Trim the embroidery to the size of the notepaper block so that the frames are central to each window. With a pair of sharp scissors, trim the inner aperture carefully, close to the stitches. Fit your picture under the frame and mount in the notepaper block according to the manufacturer's instructions.

NOTEPAPER BLOCK CHART

CHART KEY

	Anchor	DMC
7	178	791
8	177	792
9	176	793
.·	175	794
=	120	3747
::	1037	3756

Note that only one of the three sides of the
notepaper block is charted. The other two
are identical. Simply leave a single fabric
block gap, and work the next side next to
the first. Repeat this for the final side.

~ ALPHABET SAMPLER ~

SATIN STITCH

ALPHABET

The focus for the next two projects is an elegant satin stitch alphabet. The Little Princess Cushion and the Alphabet Sampler use the same techniques as the previous three projects but being larger, require more care. The use of metallic blending filament is introduced here, stitched with the stranded cotton.

MATERIALS
28 count Zweigart Quaker Evenweave fabric in Wedgwood blue 22 x 20in (56 x 50cm)

Stranded cottons as listed in the key

Tapestry needles size 24 and 22

Frame and mount of your choice (see Framing page 126)

This alphabet sampler with its pretty hedgerow border is a delight to stitch for anyone who loves cross stitch and wishes to extend their skills. The design could be worked using a different fabric or with alternative colours to make it suitable for any room in the house. The smooth stranded cotton gives the elegant satin stitch letters a look of stitched calligraphy.

WORKING THE EMBROIDERY

1 ☒ Mount the fabric into an embroidery hoop or frame and use a waste knot with a long thread to start (see Cross Stitch Basic Techniques page 11). Following the chart on pages 64–65 begin by stitching the cross stitch hedgerow border, using a size 24 tapestry needle and two strands of stranded cotton. If you have difficulty following the charts, photocopy them and stick them together with adhesive tape (there is no overlap).

2 ☒ The squares on the chart represent areas to be stitched as blocks of French knots (see Cross

Stitch Basic Techniques page 9). For these use two strands of stranded cotton and a size 24 tapestry needle. The backstitch (see Cross Stitch Basic Techniques page 9) is worked using one strand of stranded cotton and a size 24 tapestry needle.

3 ☒ Once all the cross stitch, French knots and backstitch is complete, work the satin stitch letters using a size 22 needle and all six strands of stranded cotton. Follow the chart and take care how you place the letters. All the satin stitches are worked vertically (if you are unsure about this refer to Satin Stitch Techniques page 52).

4 ☒ When all the embroidery is finished, cut off any waste knots, threading any 'tails' onto a needle and passing the thread through the back of a few stitches. Now wash and carefully press the work, right side down on a thick, fluffy towel.

5 ☒ To complete the piece see Framing page 126.

~ LITTLE PRINCESS CUSHION ~

MATERIALS
*14 count Aida in white,
16in (40cm) square*

Stranded cotton as listed in the key

*Kreinik metallic blending filament
in blue (051HL)*

Tapestry needles size 22 and 24

*Backing fabric for cushion,
14in (35cm) square*

Cushion pad, 12in (30cm) square

*Ribbon of your choice
for the bow*

This cushion makes an ideal present for the special little girl in your family as the initial can be changed to personalise the gift. The use of Kreinik metallic thread gives a touch of sparkle to your cross stitch.

WORKING THE EMBROIDERY

1 ⊠ Mount the Aida in an embroidery hoop or frame. Thread a size 24 tapestry needle with one strand of the blending filament (BF) together with two strands of stranded cotton. Following the chart on pages 62–63, start with a waste knot with a long thread (see Cross Stitch Basic Techniques page 11) and begin the cross stitching at the bottom of the fabric, leaving 3¹/₂in (9cm) unworked at the bottom for turning later.

2 ⊠ Work the squares on the chart (the blackberries) as a block of French knots (see Cross Stitch Basic Techniques page 9), using two strands of stranded cotton and a size 24 tapestry needle. Work the backstitch (see Cross Stitch Basic Techniques page 9) using one strand of stranded cotton.

3 ⊠ Now stitch the initial of your choice in satin stitch, using the alphabet from the Alphabet Sampler on pages 64–65. Use all six strands of the stranded cotton and a size 22 tapestry needle (see Satin Stitch Techniques page 52).

4 ⊠ When all the embroidery is finished, cut off any waste knots, threading any 'tails' onto a needle and passing the thread through the back of a few stitches.

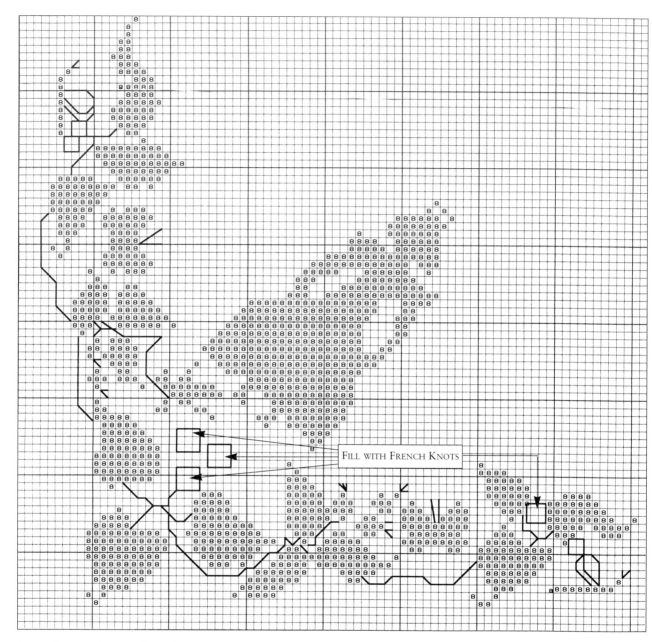

FILL WITH FRENCH KNOTS

LITTLE PRINCESS CUSHION CROSS STITCH CHART

MAKING UP THE CUSHION
1 ▣ Wash and carefully press the work, right side down on a thick, fluffy towel.

2 ▣ Trim the embroidered piece down to 13 x 9¹/2in (33 x 24cm) – this includes the 3¹/2in (9cm) allowance at the bottom. Keep the unworked piece of Aida that you

have trimmed off. Neaten the raw edge at the bottom of the embroidered piece and turn it up to the back of the embroidery, so that this now becomes a flap. Press in place.

3 ▣ The piece of unworked Aida now becomes the bottom half of the cushion front. This is done by

placing it a little under the flap and tacking the pieces together at the sides so that they become one square-shaped piece.

4 ▣ Taking the 14in (35cm) square piece of backing fabric, place it right sides together with the embroidered square. Pin, tack and then sew around the edges making

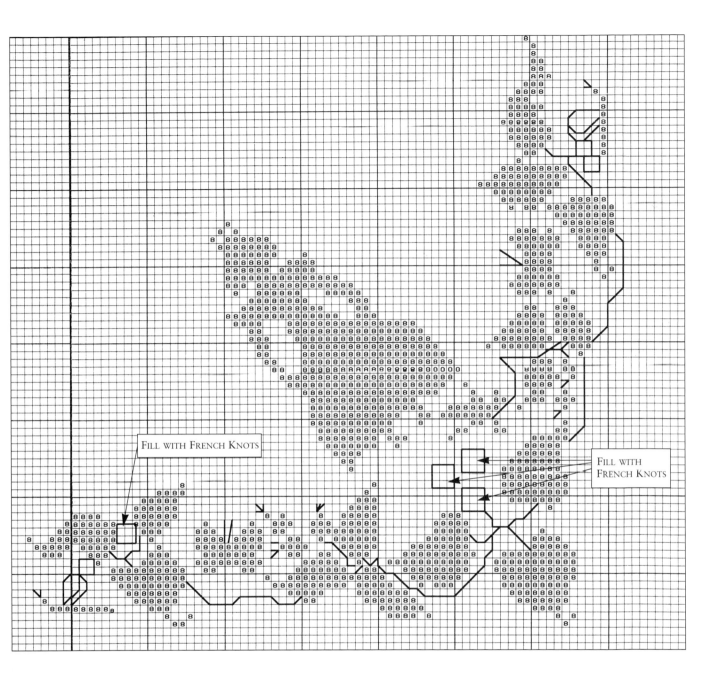

FILL WITH FRENCH KNOTS

FILL WITH
FRENCH KNOTS

sure that you leave an opening big
enough for turning and inserting
the cushion pad.

5 ▨ Remove the pins and tacking,
then trim the excess fabric, clip the
corners and turn the work through
to the right side. Press carefully,
right side down on a thick,
fluffy towel.

6 ▨ Insert the cushion pad and
slipstitch the opening closed. Add a
satin ribbon to tie the flap securely
with a bow. We also added four
tassels as decoration (see Finishing
Techniques page 127).

CHART KEY

	Anchor	DMC
8	147	797 + BF 051HL

Backstitch

	Anchor	DMC
—	147	797

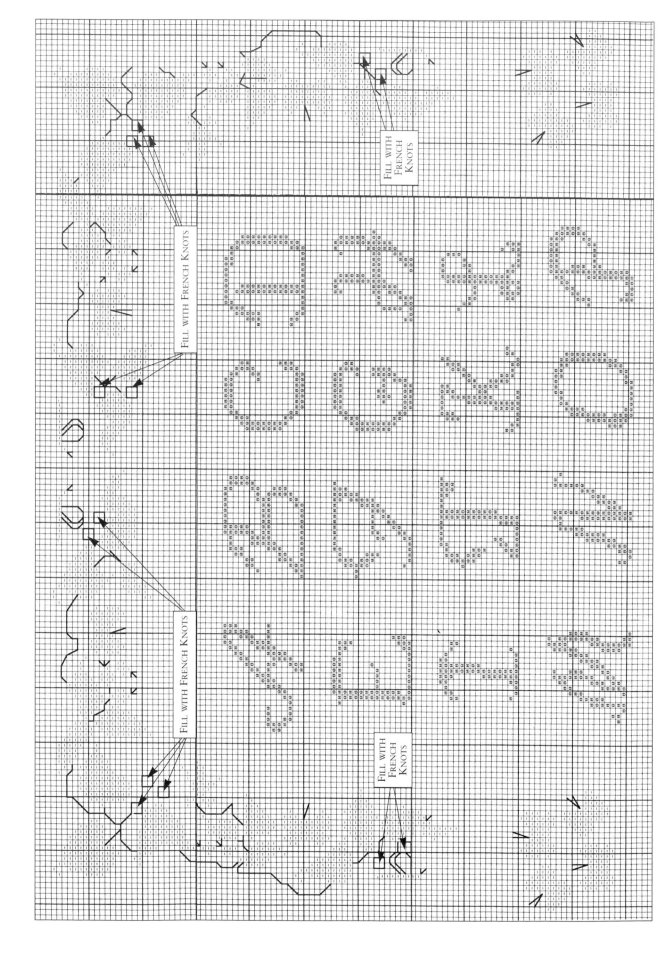

FILL WITH FRENCH KNOTS

FILL WITH FRENCH KNOTS

FILL WITH FRENCH KNOTS

FILL WITH FRENCH KNOTS

64

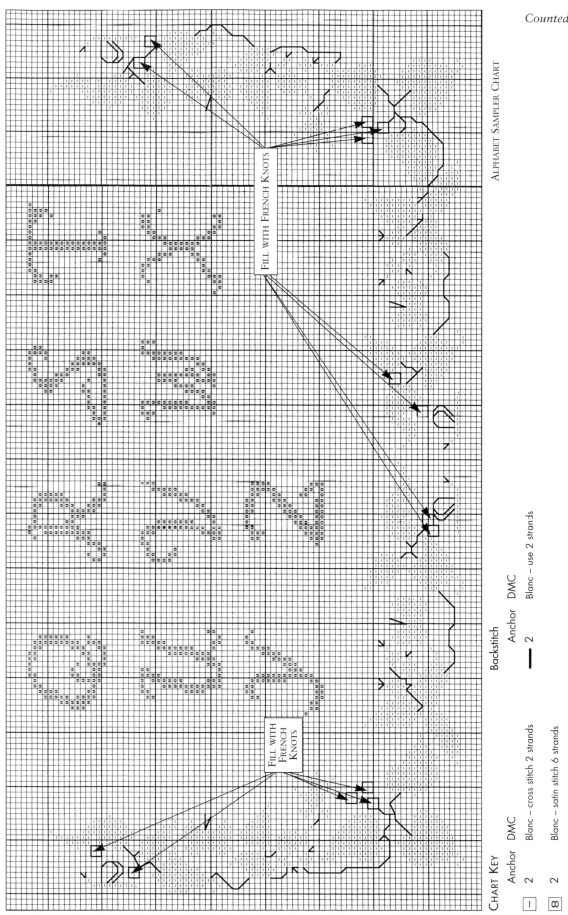

ALPHABET SAMPLER CHART

FILL WITH FRENCH KNOTS

FILL WITH FRENCH KNOTS

Backstitch

Anchor   DMC

— 2   Blanc – use 2 strands

CHART KEY

Anchor   DMC

2   Blanc – cross stitch 2 strands

2   Blanc – satin stitch 6 strands

| - |

| 8 |

~ BROWN BEAR FOOTSTOOL ~

PICTURESQUE

PATTERNS

The advanced and final project in this chapter, a beautifully patterned footstool, combines satin stitch and cross stitch perfectly, allowing you to practice and perfect the techniques. Using pearl cottons and space-dyed threads, the embroidery is both richly decorated and yet practical.

MATERIALS

20 count Zweigart Bellana Evenweave fabric in cream, 21in (53cm) square

Pearl cottons No.5 as listed in the key

Caron Watercolours threads as listed in the key

Tapestry needle size 22

Footstool (see Suppliers page 127)

The inspiration for this colourful design came from the magnificent wildlife of north-west America and Canada. The motifs of pine trees and wild salmon can be seen in the satin stitch and brown bears in the cross stitch.

WORKING THE EMBROIDERY

1 ▣ Mount the fabric into an embroidery hoop or frame and start in the centre with a waste knot with a long thread (see Cross Stitch Basic Techniques page 11). Following the charts on pages 68–69, work the central band of cross stitch using one strand of pearl cotton and a size 22 tapestry needle.

2 ▣ Once the first band of cross stitch has been stitched, follow the satin stitch chart to work the bands above and below this using half lengths to stop the thread from becoming fuzzy. Starting on the left-hand side, the satin stitch chart repeats across the band, continuing the pattern.

3 ▣ Stitch the next two cross stitch bands followed by the satin stitch bands and so on. The work grows out from the centre. When all the embroidery is finished, cut off any waste knots, threading any 'tails' onto a needle and passing through the back of a few stitches.

4 ▣ Once all complete wash and gently press your work, right side down on a thick towel.

5 ▣ To mount the embroidery in the footstool see Finishing Techniques page 126.

BROWN BEAR FOOTSTOOL COUNTED SATIN STITCH CHARTS

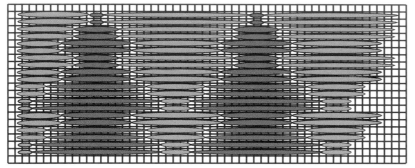

BAND A

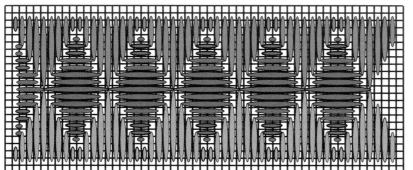

BAND B

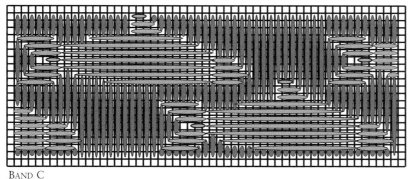

BAND C

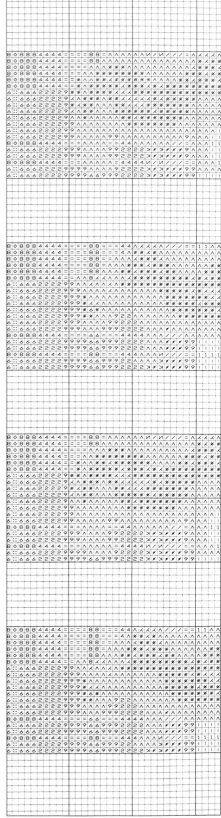

SATIN STITCH CHART KEY

Caron watercolours

▨	Fuschia
▨	Marigold
▨	Burnt toast

CROSS STITCH CHART KEY

	Anchor	DMC		Anchor	DMC
ꟷ	871	3041	⊬	306	725
1	869	3743	◇	305	743
2	896	3722	✔	44	815
4	894	224	/	338	356
6	862	935	И	778	948
8	843	3012	∧	310	780
9	150	336	✕	349	301
=	162	825	⟋	347	402
∷	308	782			

BROWN BEAR FOOTSTOOL CROSS STITCH CHART

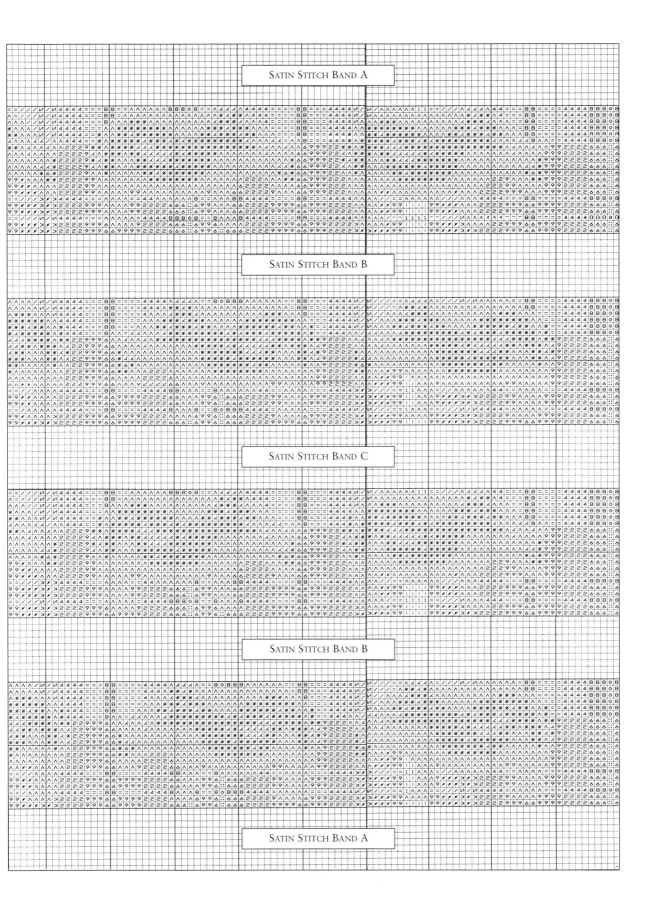

SATIN STITCH BAND A

SATIN STITCH BAND B

SATIN STITCH BAND C

SATIN STITCH BAND B

SATIN STITCH BAND A

CROSS STITCH PLUS
BLACKWORK

Blackwork is a type of embroidery characterised by black stitching on white fabric. It is generally thought to have been popularised in England in the sixteenth century by Katharine of Aragon, who came to England from Spain to marry Henry VIII in 1509, although there is evidence to suggest that the embroidery existed in England even earlier. Blackwork is sometimes called Spanish work because of this link with Katharine of Aragon. She brought with her a love of embroidery and popularised the fashionable Spanish style for stitching black on white. The embroidery was used to embellish costume accessories such as ruffs, cuffs and sleeves and it continued to be popular throughout the Elizabethan age.

Black silk thread for the stitching was imported from the eastern Mediterranean via the Netherlands and the fabric most often used was bleached white linen as this made a good contrast. The range of stitches used was very large, some of the most popular being backstitch, chain stitch, plaited braid stitch, buttonhole stitch and double running stitch (also known as Holbein stitch). The black thread was often embellished with metal threads, usually in the form of silver-gilt or vermeil. Spangles or sequins were also added and held in place with a black silk retaining stitch or a French knot. Although immensely popular in its time, the art of blackwork fell out of favour in this country in the seventeenth century until it was revived in the early twentieth century. The Embroiderers' Guild have many good examples of this more recent work.

In this chapter we have chosen to concentrate on two main stitches for blackwork which are the most suitable for use with counted thread work – backstitch and double running (Holbein) stitch. The patterns created when stitching blackwork can range from dense to very fine and lacy and complement cross stitch perfectly. Used in this way it is an ideal form of stitching to mix with cross stitch as once the outlines have been counted and stitched the filling patterns are simply repeated throughout the space.

BLACKWORK ▣ BASIC TECHNIQUES

BACKSTITCH

Backstitch is one of the most common stitches in blackwork and can be used for outlines and filling stitches.

1 ▣ Start by using a waste knot placed in the path of your stitches (see page 11), and come up through the fabric a few stitches from it.

2 ▣ Make the first stitch backwards. Pass the needle down through the fabric, a little in front of the first stitch and make another stitch inserting the needle at the point where it first came through. Repeat this step so that the stitches made pass over the thread from the waste knot. Once you have stitched about four stitches and the waste thread is caught in, it can be trimmed.

3 ▣ Continue stitching neatly and evenly. You should always be stitching backwards over a stitch that you have already made (see Figure 1). Try not to pull on the thread as this will make the stitches too small.

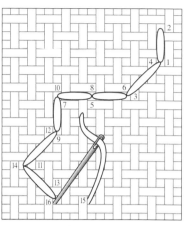

FIGURE 1

DOUBLE RUNNING STITCH (OR HOLBEIN STITCH)

This stitch can also be used in blackwork but we advise that it is only used for the outlines. The back of the fabric will look the same as the front of the work when worked in straight lines with no gaps. It is not recommended for the filling patterns, as with the lacier patterns there are a lot of gaps and this will mean that the back of the work will not look the same as the front.

1 ▣ Start by using a waste knot with a long thread, (see page 11), placed away from the path of your stitches. Work a line of simple evenly-spaced running stitches.

2 ▣ Once you have reached the end of the row you will now have a straight line of stitches with gaps between them (see Figure 2a). Make the last stitch and turn back on yourself, making a simple running stitch in the opposite direction, filling in the gaps (see Figures 2c and 2d).

3 ▣ Now neaten the ends of the stitching by threading the ends of any threads at the reverse of the

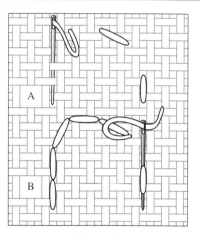

FIGURE 2

work carefully back a little way along the stitched line before trimming them.

STITCHING BLACKWORK ON DIFFERENT FABRICS

Aida When stitching blackwork on Aida fabric, the stitches are made by passing a thread over a single fabric block (see Figures 4 and 5).

Evenweave When stitching blackwork on evenweave fabric, the stitches are made by passing the thread over two fabric threads (see Figure 3).

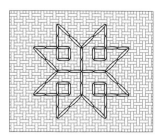

FIGURE 3

USING A CHART

The blackwork charts are combined with the cross stitch charts and are followed in the same way. The blackwork stitches are repre-sented by straight lines. The key indicates the type, colour and number of strands of thread to be used.

ORDER OF STITCHING

When stitching blackwork it is always best to stitch the outline stitches first. These are stitched in coton à broder to give a slightly thicker line and can be stitched in backstitch or double running (Holbein) stitch. Once the outline is completed the filling patterns can be repeated throughout the empty spaces. These are usually stitched using one strand of stranded cotton in backstitch.

When working the filling patterns one way of stitching is to work out the shortest journey that the thread has to make for each motif and then repeat that journey throughout the pattern, as this makes fewer loops at the back of the work (see Figures 4a–4d). To use this method, follow and repeat the backstitch number sequence shown on Figure 4a.

Some people however prefer to work all the horizontals, verticals and diagonals of a pattern in sequence as shown in Figures 5a–5d. A number sequence is suggested here too.

This method is also valid and really, the order of stitching a filling pattern can be left entirely to personal preference.

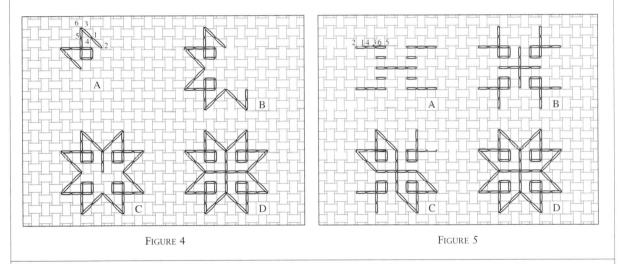

FIGURE 4   FIGURE 5

BLACKWORK ◪ TOOLS OF THE TRADE

THREADS

The following threads have been used in this chapter.

Stranded cotton Stranded cotton thread is a six-ply mercerised cotton available in vast colour range. The cotton can be separated into six individual strands and it's with a single strand that we stitch the fine blackwork filling patterns.

Coton à broder Coton à broder is a single-ply cotton that is available in six different weights, No.16 being used in this chapter. It is a fine thread and only one strand is used when stitching.

Blending filament Blending filament is a fine metallic thread which is combined with a stranded cotton to add a shine or highlight to a stitch. There are various ranges on the market, available in different colours and weights. We have used the Kreinik range. To use a metallic blending filament first separate the stranded cotton into the correct number of strands then add the same length of blending filament, threading both into the needle. It is recommend that you use a fairly short length of thread as this helps prevent tangling and stretching of the filament.

~ *H A N D B A G   M I R R O R* ~

DELICATE

BEGINNINGS

To introduce you to blackwork we have chosen three beautifully delicate designs – a handbag mirror, a powder compact and a pincushion. Each piece is both decorative and practical and are easy to do. We have used coloured thread for the blackwork stitches of these designs. This is not traditional in blackwork but shows some of the wonderful effects that can be achieved when working this type of embroidery with cross stitch.

MATERIALS
14 count Zweigart Aida in white, 7in (17.5cm) square

Stranded cottons as listed in the key

Tapestry needle size 24

Iron-on Vilene 7in (17.5cm) square

Framecraft handbag mirror (see Suppliers page 127)

The delicate floral design on this dainty mirror makes a perfect partner for the powder compact. Although you might think it is too precious to put away in a handbag the layer of clear acetate over the top acts as a perfect protection for the embroidery.

WORKING THE EMBROIDERY
1 ⊠ Mount the fabric in a small hoop or frame and following the chart on page 77 begin the cross stitch with a waste knot in the centre of the fabric (see Cross Stitch Basic Techniques page 11). Work the cross stitch using two strands of stranded cotton and a size 24 tapestry needle.

2 ⊠ Once all the cross stitch is completed, stitch the blackwork using two strands of stranded

cotton and a size 24 needle. The placement of the backstitches is indicated by the black lines on the chart. The outer circular line denotes the circle edge and is not a stitching line.

3 ⊠ Once all the stitching is complete, wash the piece and press face down into a fluffy towel. Stabilise the embroidery at this stage by pressing the piece of iron-on Vilene on to the back of the work.

4 ⊠ Mount the embroidered piece in the mirror following the manufacturer's instructions. For photographic reasons we have not mounted the acetate in the mirror, however we suggest that you do use it.

~ POWDER COMPACT ~

14 count Zweigart Aida in white, 7in (17.5cm) square

Stranded cottons as listed in the key

Tapestry needle size 24

Iron-on Vilene 7in (17.5cm) square

Framecraft powder compact (see Suppliers page 127)

The fine blackwork patterns of this design were inspired by a sixteenth century blackwork design on a neck ruff, which was beautifully embroidered with tiny lacy patterns. With its matching mirror, the powder compact is sure to conjure up images of a bygone age.

WORKING THE EMBROIDERY

1 ⊠ Mount the fabric in a small hoop or frame and following the chart below begin the cross stitch with a waste knot in the centre of the fabric (see Cross Stitch Basic Techniques page 11). Work the cross stitch using two strands of stranded cotton and a size 24 tapestry needle.

2 ⊠ Once all the cross stitch is completed stitch the blackwork

using two strands of stranded cotton and a size 24 needle. The placement of the backstitches is indicated by the black lines on the chart. The outer circular line denotes the circle edge and is *not* a stitching line.

3 ⊠ Once all the stitching is complete wash the piece and press face down into a fluffy towel. Stabilise the embroidery at this stage by pressing the piece of iron-on Vilene on to the back.

4 ⊠ Mount the embroidered piece in the powder compact following the manufacturer's instructions. For photographic reasons we have not mounted the acetate in the compact, however we suggest that you do use it.

CHART KEY

	Anchor	DMC
I	305	743
⊠	306	725
▽	265	471
∃	264	3348
✳	293	727
●	95	3609
Ⅱ	96	3608
▼	98	553

Blackwork
| ─ | 101 | 550 |

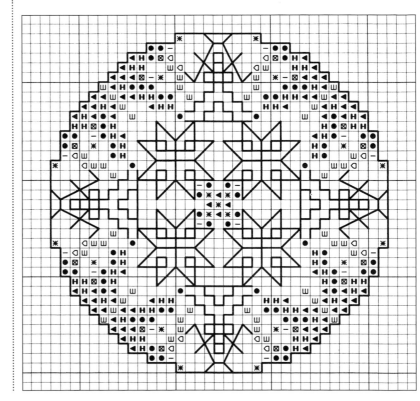

~ PINCUSHION ~

MATERIALS

14 count Zweigart Aida in white, 7in (17.5cm) square

Stranded cottons as listed in the key

Tapestry needle size 24

Pincushion with wooden base (see Suppliers page 127)

Fine thread for mounting the pincushion

Sewing pins

The fancy, delicate design for this pincushion was inspired by a pattern on an old blackwork sampler. Although the design may look very complicated for a beginner's piece it is in fact only one simple design repeated sixteen times, creating a fine lacy, effect.

WORKING THE EMBROIDERY

1 ⊠ Mount the fabric in a small hoop or frame and following the chart provided (right) begin the cross stitch with a waste knot in the centre of the fabric (see Cross Stitch Basic Techniques, page 11). Work the cross stitch using two strands of stranded cotton and a size 24 tapestry needle.

2 ⊠ Once all the cross stitch is completed, stitch the blackwork using one strand of stranded cotton and a size 24 tapestry needle. The placement of the backstitches is indicated by the black lines on the chart. The outer circular line denotes the circle edge and is *not* a stitching line.

3 ⊠ Once all the stitching is complete, wash the piece and press face down into a fluffy towel.

4 ⊠ To mount the embroidery into the pincushion, place it over the pad of the pincushion and trim around the edge 1in (2.5cm) from the stitching. With the piece positioned correctly over the pad use a few pins to hold it in place. With fine thread and a size 24 needle, anchor the thread at the back of the piece, making small running stitches around the edge until all the circumference has been stitched. Gather the thread around the pad until the embroidery fits snugly. You may need to add a few securing stitches across the back to pull it in tightly. Remove the pins.

5 ⊠ Now mount your pad in the wooden base of the pincushion and use the screw provided to secure it.

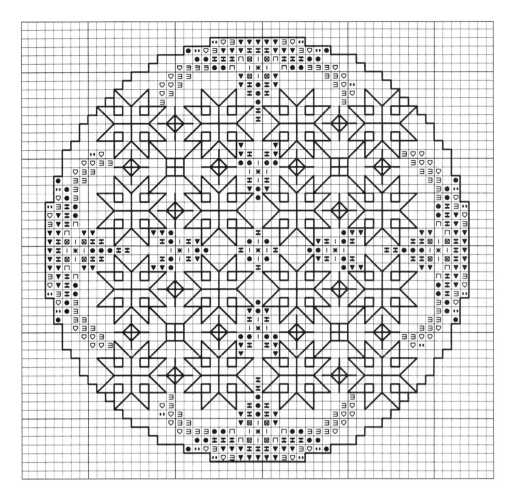

PINCUSHION CHART

CHART KEY

	Anchor	DMC
I	305	743
⊠	306	725
˙˙	266	470
▽	265	471
Ǝ	264	3348
⊓	87	3607
✳	293	727
●	95	3609
ⲁ	96	3608
▼	98	553

Blackwork

▬	101	550

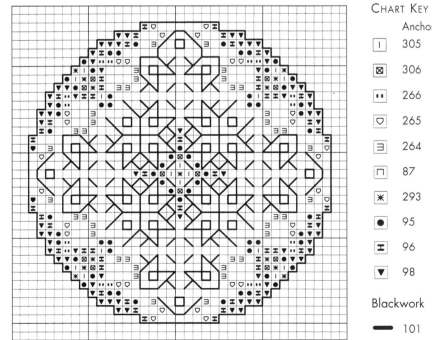

HANDBAG MIRROR CHART

~ CASTLE PICTURE ~

BUILDING SKILLS

*This section introduces many
of the more typical stitching
patterns used in blackwork and
also uses two different weights
of thread. The stitching of the
key outer lines is done in coton
à broder and is always best
completed first, leaving blocks
of blank fabric which can then
be filled in with the patterns
stitched in one strand of
stranded cotton.*

MATERIALS

*14 count Zweigart Aida in white,
12 x 14in (30.5 x 35.5cm)*

Stranded cottons as listed in the key

Coton à broder No. 16 in black

Tapestry needle size 24

Frame of your choice

*This imposing castle design includes
many of the traditional patterns that
have been used over the ages in
counted forms of blackwork. It is not
so hard to imagine that four hundred
years ago a lady may have sat in a
castle such as this embroidering
similar patterns onto her sampler.*

WORKING THE EMBROIDERY

1 ⊠ Mount the fabric in a hoop or
frame and following the chart
provided (right), begin the cross
stitch with a waste knot (see Cross
Stitch Basic Techniques page 11).
Work the cross stitch using two
strands of stranded cotton and a size
24 tapestry needle.

2 ⊠ Once all the cross stitch is
completed you can begin the
blackwork. The placement of the
blackwork stitches is indicated by

the two different types of lines on
the chart. The darker lines are
stitched in coton à broder and the
lighter ones indicate the blackwork
patterned stitches (as indicated in
the key). Stitch the outer lines of the
blackwork design using one strand
of coton à broder and a size 24
needle where indicated on the chart.
Then stitch the blackwork patterns
using one strand of black stranded
cotton and a size 24 needle. It is
much easier to stitch the thick lines
first and then fill in the spaces with
each of the different patterns.

3 ⊠ Once all the stitching is
complete wash the piece and press
face down into a fluffy towel.

4 ⊠ Mount your piece in a frame
of your choice (see Finishing
Techniques page 126).

Blackwork Castle Chart

Chart Key

	Anchor	DMC			Anchor	DMC
◸	265	471		◹	211	986
△	266	470		→	210	562
◼	267	469		↑	281	732

Blackwork

━━ Black coton à broder

━━ 403

79

~ FAERY PICTURE ~

MAGICAL EFFECTS

In this advanced design, with its more intricate blackwork filling patterns, we have used stranded cottons, coton à broder, metallic threads and spangles or sequins to convey the richness found in some traditional blackwork. The piece has been worked on a dark-coloured fabric with light-coloured threads for the border, but if you prefer a more authentic blackwork border you could use black threads and a light-coloured fabric.

MATERIALS
14 count Zweigart Aida in dark blue, 24 x 28in (61 x 71cm)

Stranded cottons as listed in the key

Coton à broder as listed in the key

Kreinik blending filament as listed in the key

Sequins as listed in the key

Tapestry needle size 24

Frame of your choice

This enchanting faery design has a fine and lacy blackwork border. The corner motifs were inspired by an iris in bloom. Traditionally, floral designs were very popular in blackwork with each flower representing a different meaning. Our faery is delicately testing the warmth of the pool with her toe.

WORKING THE EMBROIDERY

1 ⊠ Mount the fabric in a hoop or frame and following the charts on page 82–85, begin the cross stitch with a waste knot (see Cross Stitch Basic Techniques, page 11). Work the cross stitch using two strands of stranded cotton and a size 24 tapestry needle. Where indicated in the key one strand of blending filament (BF) should be combined with two strands of stranded cotton. (See page 73 for how to stitch using metallic thread.)

2 ⊠ Once all the cross stitch is completed you can begin the blackwork. The placement of the blackwork stitches is indicated by the different coloured lines on the chart. Follow the backstitch key and where indicated use one strand of the coton à broder or stranded cotton using a size 24 needle. Work the coton à broder first, then stitch the blackwork patterns. It is much easier to stitch the thick lines first and then fill in the spaces with each of the different patterns.

3 ⊠ Following the chart, stitch on the sequins using four strands of stranded cotton and a size 24 needle. Their position on the embroidery is indicated by the small, red crosses. Secure each one with a French knot in the central hole (see page 9 for how to work French knots).

4 ⊠ Once all the stitching is complete wash the piece and press face down into a fluffy towel.

5 ⊠ Mount your embroidery in a frame of your choice (see Finishing Techniques page 126).

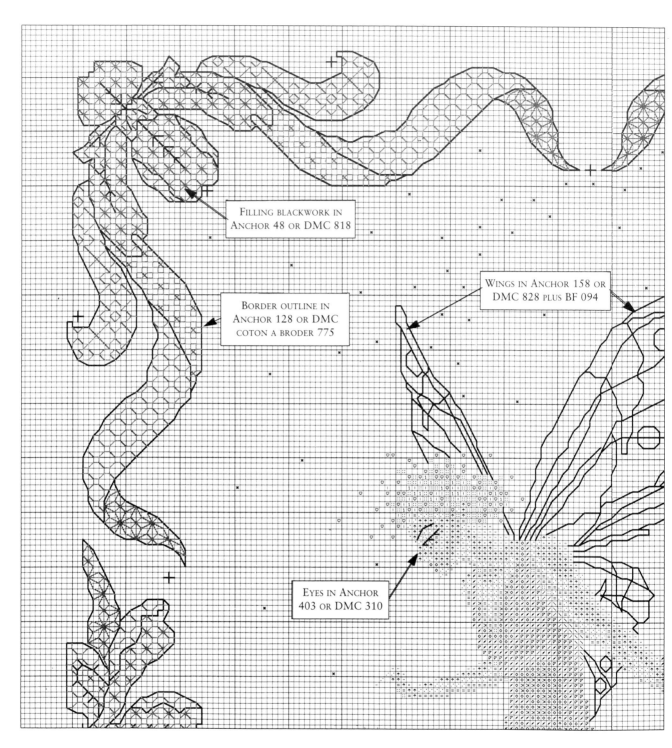

FILLING BLACKWORK IN
ANCHOR 48 OR DMC 818

WINGS IN ANCHOR 158 OR
DMC 828 PLUS BF 094

BORDER OUTLINE IN
ANCHOR 128 OR DMC
COTON A BRODER 775

EYES IN ANCHOR
403 OR DMC 310

FAERY PICTURE CHART PART 1

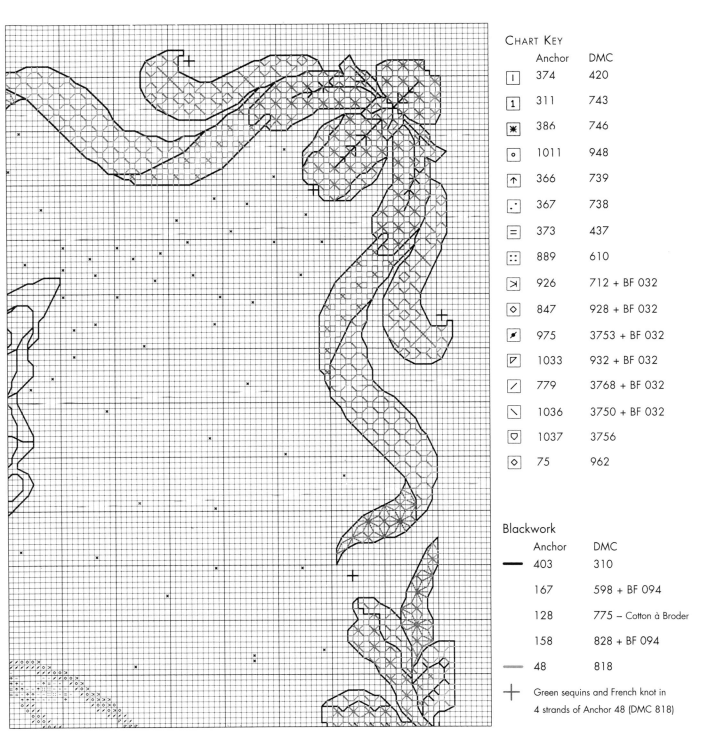

CHART KEY

	Anchor	DMC
I	374	420
1	311	743
✳	386	746
o	1011	948
↑	366	739
∴	367	738
=	373	437
∷	889	610
⊠	926	712 + BF 032
◇	847	928 + BF 032
◤	975	3753 + BF 032
▽	1033	932 + BF 032
/	779	3768 + BF 032
\	1036	3750 + BF 032
▽	1037	3756
◇	75	962

Blackwork

	Anchor	DMC
—	403	310
	167	598 + BF 094
	128	775 – Cotton à Broder
	158	828 + BF 094
—	48	818
+	Green sequins and French knot in 4 strands of Anchor 48 (DMC 818)	

NOTE:

This chart is in two parts and is produced here over four pages (pages 82 to 85). You may find it easier to photocopy all the parts and stick them together carefully to make one complete chart before you begin to stitch.

FILLING BLACKWORK IN
ANCHOR 48 OR DMC 818

BORDER OUTLINE IN
ANCHOR 128 OR DMC
COTON A BRODER 775

POOL IN ANCHOR 167 OR
DMC 598 PLUS BF 094

FAERY PICTURE CHART PART 2

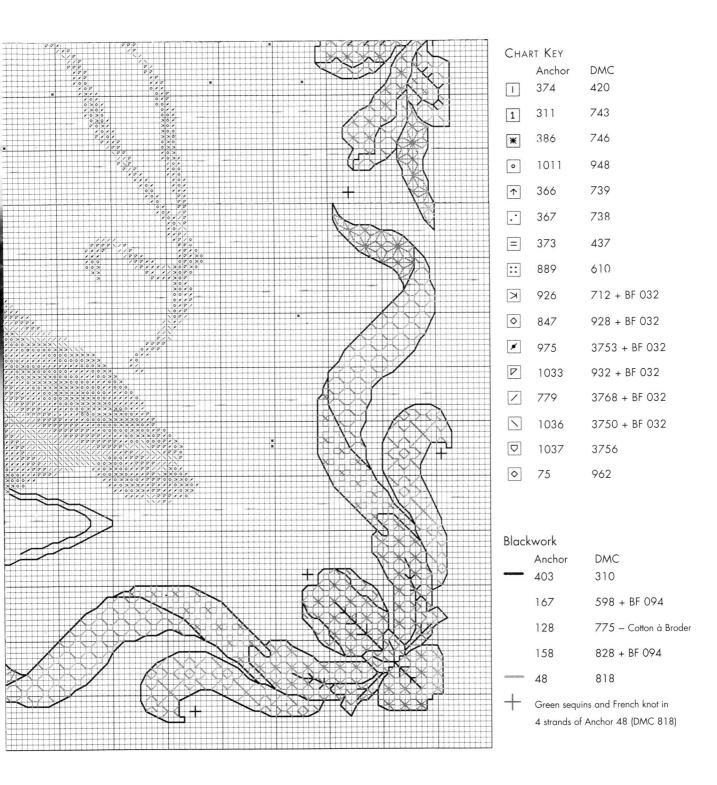

CHART KEY

	Anchor	DMC
I	374	420
1	311	743
✳	386	746
o	1011	948
↑	366	739
.·	367	738
=	373	437
∷	889	610
⋈	926	712 + BF 032
◇	847	928 + BF 032
◢	975	3753 + BF 032
▽	1033	932 + BF 032
╱	779	3768 + BF 032
╲	1036	3750 + BF 032
▽	1037	3756
◈	75	962

Blackwork

	Anchor	DMC
▬	403	310
	167	598 + BF 094
	128	775 – Cotton à Broder
	158	828 + BF 094
▬	48	818
+	Green sequins and French knot in 4 strands of Anchor 48 (DMC 818)	

CROSS STITCH PLUS
HARDANGER

*This beautiful type of embroidery is believed to have
been created when a Norwegian sailor brought back a piece of
embroidery from Persia to his wife in Hardanger, a town situated
on a fjord in Norway. Over many years the Hardanger embroidery
we know today was developed. The thread and fabric are much
more substantial than the Persian version but the resemblance
can still be seen, noticeably the tradition of using
white thread on white fabric.*

*Hardanger is a geometric form of counted
embroidery and traditionally the stitching is done with white
thread on a white background. Satin stitch blocks, known as
Kloster blocks, are stitched in different patterns to create
enclosed areas which then are cut and removed. These
holes are decorated with intricate filling stitches in fine
thread forming an overall lacy appearance.*

*Many of the Hardanger motifs have a nautical theme – not
surprising for a sea-faring nation like Norway. The national
costume in the Hardanger region has beautifully embroidered
aprons and even the men wear embellished cravats. Recently
Hardanger designs have become more and more lacy
and delicate in appearance and these look particularly intricate
when stitched on fine linen fabric. Changing the colour of
the fabric or thread creates a very different image and
atmosphere to the embroidery and allows you to
create your own look.*

*Hardanger embroidery combines beautifully with
cross stitch and is a natural progression for the cross stitch
lover who is looking for a new stitching dimension.
As in cross stitch, the charts are easy to follow and
once the basic techniques are mastered the work grows
quickly, making it practical even for larger items
such as tablecloths or duvet covers.*

HARDANGER ▣ BASIC TECHNIQUES

HARDANGER CHARTS AND STITCHING ORDER

The projects in this chapter have two charts – a Hardanger chart and a cross stitch chart.

When following the Hardanger chart it is important to remember that one line on the chart represents a woven fabric thread. The blocks of satin stitch or Kloster blocks are shown clearly on the charts, forming enclosed areas that can be cut and decorated with lacy filling stitches. Areas where threads need to be cut are marked with a plain black square.

To achieve the best effects in Hardanger embroidery, the order of stitching is important, so in general try to follow the order of working given below.

1 *Kloster blocks.*
2 *Eyelet stitches.*
3 *Other surface stitchery, ie heart, ship, star motifs.*
4 *Cutting threads.*
5 *Other filling stitches, ie dove's eye and square filling stitch.*

KLOSTER BLOCKS

Kloster blocks are one of the most important motifs in Hardanger embroidery. Traditionally, five stitches are worked over four threads of the fabric, as follows.

1 ▣ Using a length of pearl cotton No.5 and a size 22 tapestry needle, start with a waste knot with a long thread (see Cross Stitch Basics Techniques page 11).

2 ▣ Figure 1 shows the order of stitching and the position on the chart. Work five vertical straight stitches over four threads of the fabric. (If you are left handed start at position 9 and work to the

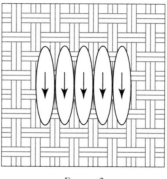

FIGURE 2

other side.) Figure 2 shows how the stitches will look on the fabric when they are completed.

3 ▣ To move on to the next block of stitches, count up four threads and insert the needle, producing a straight stitch, not a diagonal one, on the back of the work.

4 ▣ Work the horizontal stitches in the same way, making sure that the stitches interlink into the corner holes (see Figure 3). This completes a Kloster block.

5 ▣ Turn the work over and fasten off by passing the needle and thread under a block of five stitches before cutting the thread

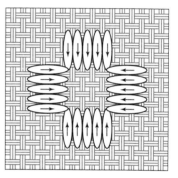

FIGURE 3

off neatly. Cut the waste knot off, then thread the 'tail' onto the needle and fasten off in the same way.

Kloster blocks

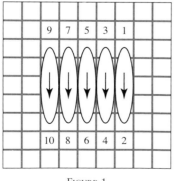

FIGURE 1

EYELET STITCH

Eyelet stitch is a filling stitch which is worked before the cutting of the threads. Eyelets are a form of straight stitch where all the stitches converge on a central point. In Hardanger work they complement the Kloster blocks.

1 ⊠ Eyelets are stitched in pearl cotton No.8 using a size 24 tapestry needle. Anchor the thread by passing it under the back of a Kloster block and securing with a small backstitch, then bring it up in the front of the work at a corner point.

2 ⊠ Starting from one corner, work each stitch in succession. Figure 4 shows the direction of the stitches into the central point. Giving an extra tug as you complete each stitch will produce a more pleasing effect overall, as a neat hole will be formed.

FIGURE 4

HEART MOTIF

The heart is an ancient symbol of love. This surface stitched motif is used throughout the designs because we love its simplicity.

1 ⊠ Using pearl cotton No.5 and a size 22 tapestry needle, start with a waste knot with a long thread (see Cross Stitch Basic Techniques page 11). Stitch the motif from one side to the other (see Figure 5).

2 ⊠ Fasten off by passing the thread through the back of the stitches. Cut the waste knot off, then thread the 'tail' onto a needle, fastening off in the same way.

3 ⊠ Fasten off the thread by securing it under the back of surrounding stitches, or pass the thread through the back of the work to start another filling stitch.

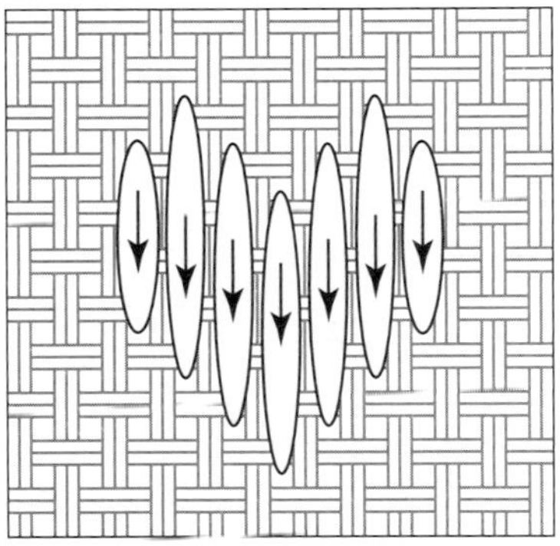

FIGURE 5

SHIP MOTIF

Ship motifs and other nautical themes are common to Persian and Norwegian embroidery. It is easy to see the hull of a ship when two of these surface stitched motifs are placed together.

1 ⊠ Using pearl cotton No.5 and a size 22 tapestry needle, start with a waste knot with a long thread (see Cross Stitch Basic Techniques page 11). Begin stitching at position 1 shown on Figure 6 and work the stitches in order.

2 ⊠ To finish off this surface stitch, carry the thread neatly up through the back of the stitches and cut off close to the work. Cut the waste knot off, then thread the 'tail' onto the needle and fasten off in the same way as before.

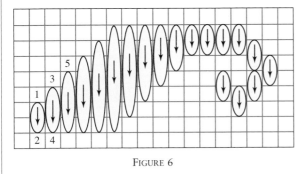

FIGURE 6

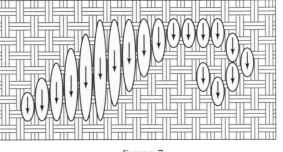

FIGURE 7

STAR MOTIF
The star motif is an effective surface stitch in Hardanger work.

1 ⊠ Using pearl cotton No.5 and a size 22 tapestry needle, start with a waste knot with a long thread (see Cross Stitch Basic Techniques page 11). Starting from one of the points shown on Figure 8 (a stitch over one thread) work your way towards the centre, following the directional arrows.

2 ⊠ Work the same way from each point. The thread carried at the back of the work will be stitched in on your way back down the point of the star.

3 ⊠ Finish off by running the thread through the stitches at the back of the work. Cut off neatly. Cut the waste knot off, then thread the 'tail' onto the needle and fasten off in the same way.

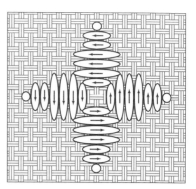

FIGURE 8

SQUARE FILLING STITCH
This is a useful filling stitch worked after the cutting of the threads to emphasise the lacy effect of the embroidery.

1 ⊠ Using pearl cotton No.8 and a size 24 tapestry needle, insert the needle into the back of the fabric where shown in Figure 9a and secure behind the surrounding stitches with a small backstitch. Put the needle through the hole and up through the fabric in the next corner, as in Figure 9b.

2 ⊠ Take the needle under the second stitch, into the hole and back out as shown in Figure 9c.

3 ⊠ Take the needle under the third stitch and over the top of the first stitch (see Figure 9d).

4 ⊠ Finish the square stitch by passing the thread through the surrounding stitches at the back, or pass through the stitches at the back on to the next filling stitch. The thread should not show on the right side.

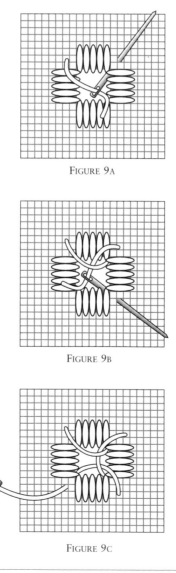

FIGURE 9A

FIGURE 9B

FIGURE 9C

FIGURE 9D

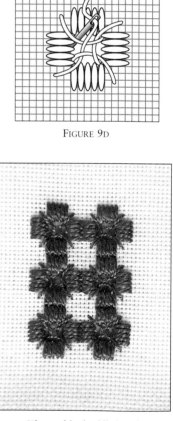

Kloster blocks filled with square filling stitches.

DOVE'S EYE FILLING STITCH

This pretty filling stitch worked after the cutting of the threads adds to the delicate cutwork quality of Hardanger work.

1 ☒ Using pearl cotton No.8 and a size 24 tapestry needle, start by securing the thread behind the surrounding stitches at the back of the work with a small backstitch. Bring the needle out of the fabric in between the stitches, as shown in Figure 10a.

2 ☒ Taking the needle over to the next side, pick up the middle stitch as shown in Figure 10b.

3 ☒ Continue round all the edges in this manner. You will see little loop stitches forming as shown in Figure 10c.

4 ☒ When you arrive back at the beginning, push the needle through the hole over the first

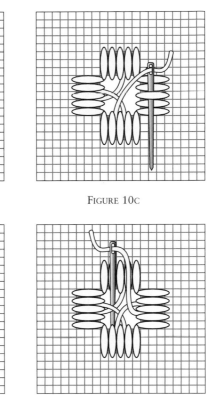

FIGURE 10A

FIGURE 10C

FIGURE 10B

FIGURE 10D

stitch you made. Then take the thread behind this stitch (see Figure 10d). Fasten off the thread

securely by passing it behind surrounding stitches or pass through to the next filling stitch.

CUTTING THREADS

There is no hard-and-fast way to cut threads in Hardanger but we use the following steps which you should find quick and easy. Don't panic – though nearly everyone does the first time they cut the fabric. Remember, if you cut your work incorrectly it can be mended. Fray a thread off the edge of the fabric and simply weave it in carefully to re-create the original weave. The areas to cut are marked with a black square.

1 ☒ Look at the work and the chart carefully before you start.

Then, open your scissors out and stick one point in the corner of the area to be cut. The point should pass through the fabric and touch your finger underneath (Figure 11).

2 ☒ Move the blade across the threads, keeping at right angles with the stitches, until you reach the corner. Snip bravely. Repeat on the opposite side of the square.

3 ☒ Using the blunt end of a needle, wheedle the threads out and remove them. You are now left with what we call piano strings.

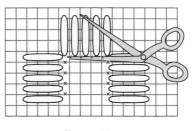

FIGURE 11

Cut these at the top then at the bottom as close as you dare. You now have a hole. Don't worry if you have hairy edges. Either trim them further or leave them as they are. When you wash your work they will tidy themselves inside the stitches.

HARDANGER ▣ TOOLS OF THE TRADE

FABRIC

There are only two points to remember when buying fabric for Hardanger work. Do *not* buy Aida fabric as it is not designed for such work and make sure the fabric is an evenweave. If you can pull a thread off the edge easily and you can see it clearly then it is suitable for Hardanger. Traditional Hardanger fabric is evenweave with 22 threads to the inch (2.5cm). If you find it difficult to see a small count fabric or working with white thread on white fabric, try using Zweigart 18 count Davosa in off-white or some other coloured Hardanger fabric.

THREADS

Traditional Hardanger embroidery is stitched in white thread, although the use of coloured thread has become more popular. This not only creates a different look but it is useful if you are a beginner to stitch in a colour, as the thread does not glare against the fabric. The thread used in Hardanger is called pearl cotton or cotton perlé, (see page 6 for more information on this thread). Generally pearl cotton No.5 is used for stitching Kloster blocks and other motifs, while pearl cotton No.8 is used for all the lacy and filling stitches.

SCISSORS

These are one of the most important pieces of equipment in Hardanger embroidery. This doesn't mean, however, that you have to buy expensive, specialised ones. All you need is a pair of sharp, small-bladed scissors. If you already have a favourite pair that you use for cross stitch and you are sure they are sharp, then use these. There are special Hardanger scissors on the market with angled blades designed to make them easier to control. Some people swear by them, others don't find them easy to use.

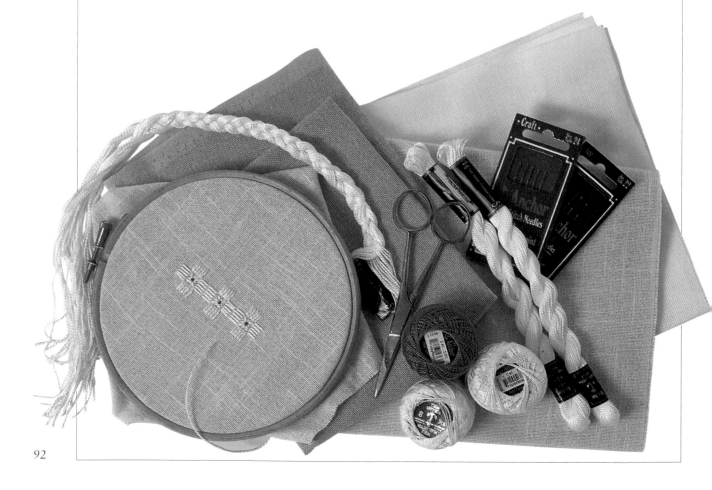

~ HEART AND STAR CARD ~

STITCHING WITHOUT CUTTING

The following three projects are ideal for those stitchers new to Hardanger embroidery. They allow you to practice and perfect some of the traditional Hardanger elements, such as Kloster blocks, eyelet stitches and the star, heart and ship surface stitches. No cutting of Hardanger threads is required for these projects.

MATERIALS
22 count Zweigart Hardanger fabric in white, 6in (15cm) square

Stranded cottons as listed in the key

Anchor pearl cotton No.5 and No.8 in white

Tapestry needles size 22 and 24

A three-fold card

Small quantity of iron-on Vilene

Double-sided adhesive tape

This versatile card would be suitable for any occasion. You could adapt it for a special birthday or anniversary by adding a message in backstitch around the edge. Apart from allowing you to practise Kloster blocks and eyelet stitches, the card features two surface stitches: the heart motif and the star motif, perhaps the same star our Norwegian sailor saw on his travels.

WORKING THE EMBROIDERY
1 ⊠ Begin by stitching the Hardanger using pearl cotton No.5 and a size 22 tapestry needle. Mount the fabric in an embroidery frame and using a waste knot with a long thread, start at the centre of the fabric (see Cross Stitch Basic Techniques page 11). Follow the chart on page 94.

2 ⊠ Stitch the Kloster blocks, then the star and heart motifs (see Hardanger Techniques page 89).

3 ⊠ Next stitch the central eyelet stitches, using pearl cotton No.8 and size 24 tapestry needle (see Hardanger Techniques page 89).

4 ⊠ Once the Hardanger stitching is complete you can begin the cross stitch. The Hardanger chart has the nearest row of stitching shown to help you place the cross stitching. The cross stitch uses three strands of stranded cotton and is stitched over two fabric threads. When all the embroidery is finished, cut off any waste knots, threading any 'tails' onto a needle and passing the thread through the back of a few stitches.

5 ⊠ Wash and press the finished embroidery. Take care not to squash the stitches by pressing face down into a thick, fluffy towel.

MAKING UP THE CARD

1 ⊠ To mount the embroidery into a card, first stabilise the embroidery with a piece of iron-on Vilene.

2 ⊠ Place the aperture of the card centrally over the embroidery to measure the size required, then trim the fabric.

3 ⊠ Put double-sided adhesive tape around the inside aperture of the card and then place over the embroidery, pressing gently to secure. Stick down the fold of the card also using tape around all edges. Personalise the card – a message inside for your special occasion.

HEART AND STAR CARD HARDANGER CHART

CROSS STITCH CHART KEY

	Anchor	DMC
I	214	966
::	238	703
⋊	258	904
◇	289	307
✗	40	957
▽	96	3608
∕	1030	3746
＼	940	792
И	139	797

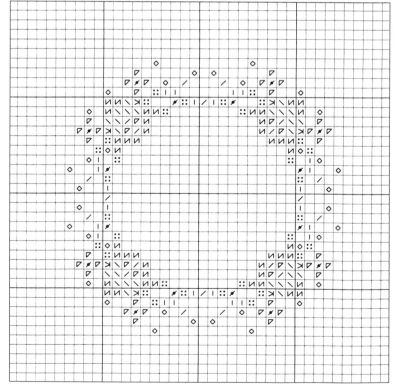

HEART AND STAR CARD CROSS STITCH CHART

~ HANGING POMANDER ~

This pretty, aromatic pomander is perfect for hanging in your wardrobe with your favourite outfit. Filled with delicately scented dried rose petals or dried peppermint and rosemary it is sure to delight each time you open the door.

WORKING THE EMBROIDERY

1 ⊠ Begin by stitching the Hardanger first. Mount one of the fabric pieces in an embroidery frame and use a waste knot with a long thread to start (see Cross Stitch Basic Techniques page 11). Use pearl cotton No.5 and a size 22 tapestry needle.

2 ⊠ Following the Hardanger chart on page 96 (remembering that one line on the chart represents a woven thread of the fabric), start by working the Kloster blocks (see Hardanger Techniques page 88).

3 ⊠ Using the same thread as for the Kloster blocks, stitch the heart motifs next (see Hardanger Basic Techniques page 89).

4 ⊠ Using pearl cotton No.8 and a size 24 tapestry needle work the eyelet stitches from the chart on page 96 (see Hardanger Basic Techniques page 89).

MATERIALS

22 count Zweigart Hardanger fabric in white, two pieces 9 x 6in (23 x 15cm)

Stranded cottons as listed in the key

Anchor pearl cotton No.5 and No.8 in white

Tapestry needles size 22 and 24

Sachet of dried herbs

Piece of ribbon for bow decoration and loop

5 ⊠ Once the Hardanger stitching is complete work the cross stitch design following the chart, using three strands of stranded cotton, stitched over two fabric threads. To help you, coloured crosses have been placed on the Hardanger chart to show where the first row of cross stitches begin. Work the top block of cross stitch first; then turn the book upside down and use the chart to work the bottom block of cross stitch. When all the embroidery is finished, cut off any waste knots, threading any 'tails' onto a needle and passing the thread through the back of a few stitches.

6 ⊠ Now wash and press your finished embroidery face down on a thick, fluffy towel.

MAKING UP THE POMANDER

1 ⊠ To make up the pomander take the other piece of Hardanger fabric and place it right sides together with the finished embroidery. Pin and tack ³⁄₈in (1cm) from the edge all round the design, leaving a small gap for turning.

2 ⊠ Stitch along the tacked line then remove the tacking and trim the edges and the corners carefully so that the sachet turns through to the right side neatly.

3 ⊠ Fill with your favourite dried herbs (finely pounded herbs may need an inner bag), then slipstitch the opening closed.

4 ⊠ With the ribbon tie a bow and make a loop. Finish by securing the bow and loop in a corner of the top edge of the pomander with a few stitches.

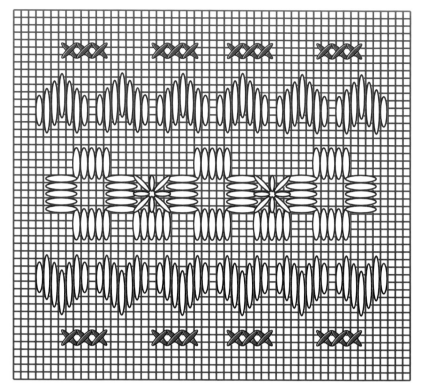

HANGING POMANDER HARDANGER CHART

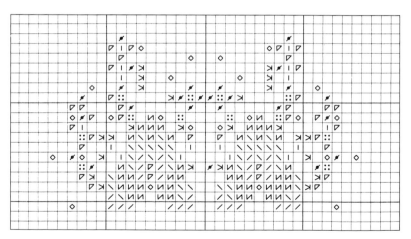

HANGING POMANDER CROSS STITCH CHART

CROSS STITCH CHART KEY

	Anchor	DMC		Anchor	DMC
I	214	966	◁	96	3608
∷	238	703	╱	1030	3746
⊣	258	904	╲	940	792
◇	289	307	И	139	797
✔	40	957			

~ SCENTED SACHET ~

This beautiful, fragrant sachet decorated with the ship motif, can be filled with perfumed herbs and is ideal to put in your favourite secret drawer. Or why not fill it with dried lavender and place it under your pillow for sweet dreams?

WORKING THE EMBROIDERY

1 ▨ Begin by stitching the Hardanger first. Mount one of the fabric squares in an embroidery frame and use a waste knot with a long thread to start (see Cross Stitch basic Techniques page 11). Use pearl cotton No.5 and a size 22 tapestry needle.

2 ▨ Following the Hardanger chart on page 98 (remembering that one line on the chart represents a woven thread of the fabric), work the Kloster blocks (see Hardanger Techniques page 88). (If you prefer to start in the centre, you could work the ship motifs first.)

3 ▨ Next work one of the central ship motifs (see Hardanger Techniques page 89) and continue until all the ship motifs are complete.

4 ▨ Using pearl cotton No.8 and a size 24 tapestry needle, work the eyelet stitches (see Hardanger Techniques page 89).

5 ▨ Once the Hardanger stitching is complete, work the cross stitch design following the chart on page 98 and using three strands of stranded cotton over two fabric threads. To help you, coloured crosses have been placed on the Hardanger chart to show where the first row of cross stitches begin. When all the embroidery is finished, cut off any waste knots, threading any 'tails' onto a needle and passing the thread through the back of a few stitches.

6 ▨ Wash and press your finished embroidery, using a thick, fluffy towel to avoid flattening the stitches.

MAKING UP THE SACHET

1 ▨ To make up the sachet take the remaining square of Hardanger fabric and place it right sides together with the embroidered square. Pin and then tack 3/8in (1cm) from the edge all around, leaving a small gap for turning.

MATERIALS
22 count Zweigart Hardanger fabric in white, two pieces 8in (20cm) square

Stranded cottons as listed in the key

Anchor pearl cotton No.5 and No.8 in white

Tapestry needles size 22 and 24

Sachet of dried herbs

Piece of ribbon for bow decoration

2 ⊠ Stitch along the tacked line then remove the tacking and trim the edges and the corners carefully so that the sachet turns through to the right side neatly.

3 ⊠ Fill with your favourite dried herbs (finely pounded herbs may need an inner bag), then slipstitch the opening closed.

4 ⊠ With the ribbon tie a bow and make a loop. Finish by securing the bow and loop in a corner of the top edge of the sachet with a few stitches.

SCENTED SACHET HARDANGER CHART

CROSS STITCH CHART KEY

	Anchor	DMC
I	214	966
∷	238	703
⇗	258	904
◇	289	307
✐	40	957
▽	96	3608
∕	1030	3746
∖	940	792
И	139	797

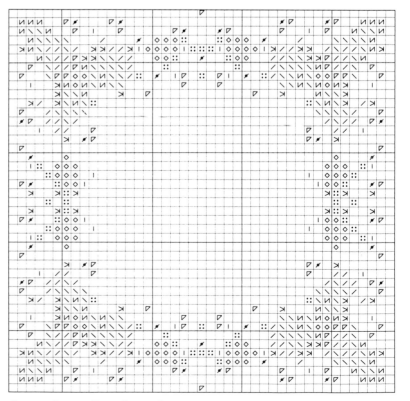

SCENTED SACHET CROSS STITCH CHART

~ SQUARE SAMPLER ~

CUTTING WITH

CONFIDENCE

The open quality and laciness achieved by cutting gives Hardanger its most distinctive feature and this square sampler is perfect for introducing you to this technique. It can be easily customised for any special occasion and is perfect for christenings, weddings, confirmations or special birthdays

MATERIALS

22 count Hardanger fabric in white, 12in (30cm) square

Stranded cottons as listed in one of the keys

Anchor pearl cotton No.5 and No.8 in white

Tapestry needles size 22, 24 and 26

A small charm of your choice

This delicate square sampler has a choice of colourways. Add a carefully chosen charm to suit the occasion, such as a gold one for a golden wedding anniversary, to make the finished piece extra special.

WORKING THE EMBROIDERY

1 ⊠ Mount the fabric in an embroidery frame and begin by stitching the cross stitch garland in the centre of the fabric, starting with a waste knot and a long thread (see Cross Stitch Basic Techniques page 11). Follow the chart on page 102 and use two strands of stranded cotton and a size 26 tapestry needle. Stitch the cross stitch over one of the fabric threads.

2 ⊠ Using one strand of stranded cotton stitch the names in backstitch (see Cross Stitch Basic

Techniques page 9) in the blank box using the alphabet below. Mark out the box onto a piece of graph paper. Mark the centre point and use this to position the middle letter of the name(s). Complete the name leaving an even gap between letters.

3 ⊠ Start the Hardanger border next. (If you're not feeling fully confident, stitch a little sample of the edge; this practice piece can be made into a gift tag later.) The Hardanger border is stitched using pearl cotton No.5 and a size 22 tapestry needle. Following the chart on page 100, stitch the Kloster blocks first (see Hardanger Basic Techniques, page 88).

4 ⊠ Using pearl cotton No.8 and a size 24 tapestry needle work the eyelet stitches (see Hardanger Basic Techniques page 89).

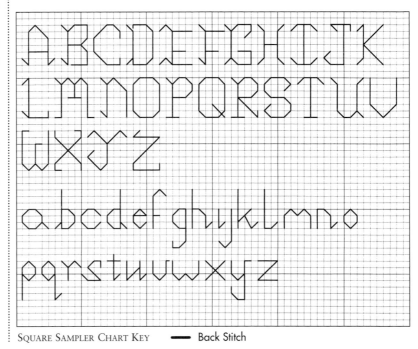

SQUARE SAMPLER CHART KEY   —— Back Stitch

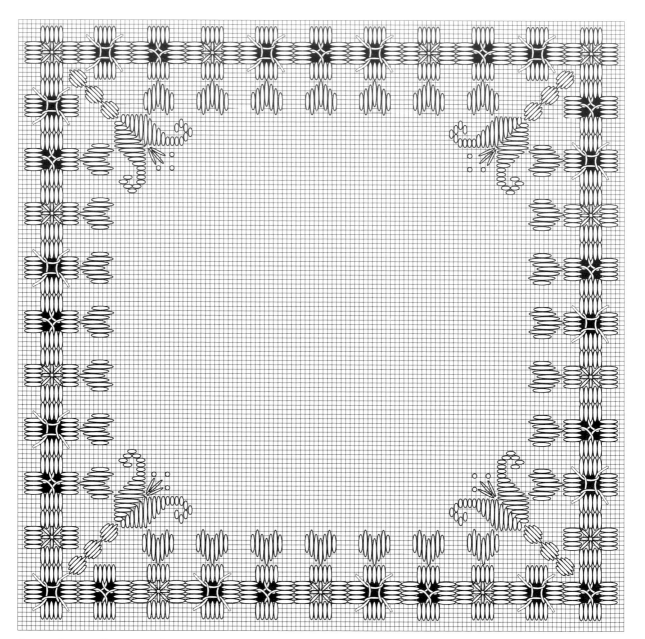

SQUARE SAMPLER HARDANGER CHART

5 ☒ Next stitch the corner motifs and hearts as shown on the chart. The dots on the chart represent French knots to be stitched using a 22 size needle and pearl cotton No.5. Complete all surface stitching before you cut anything. This enables you to correct mistakes and keep the tension even.

6 ☒ Cut the Hardanger fabric threads next, these are the black squares on the chart (see Hardanger Basic Techniques page 91).

7 ☒ Stitch the dove's eyes and square filling stitches next (see Hardanger Basic Techniques page 90), using pearl cotton No.8 and a size 24 tapestry needle. Start in the top left-hand corner. When finished,

cut off any waste knots, threading 'tails' onto a needle and passing through the back of a few stitches.

8 ☒ Wash your sampler then press it face down on a thick, fluffy towel.

9 ☒ Place the small charm in position and stitch into place. The sampler is now ready for framing (see page 126).

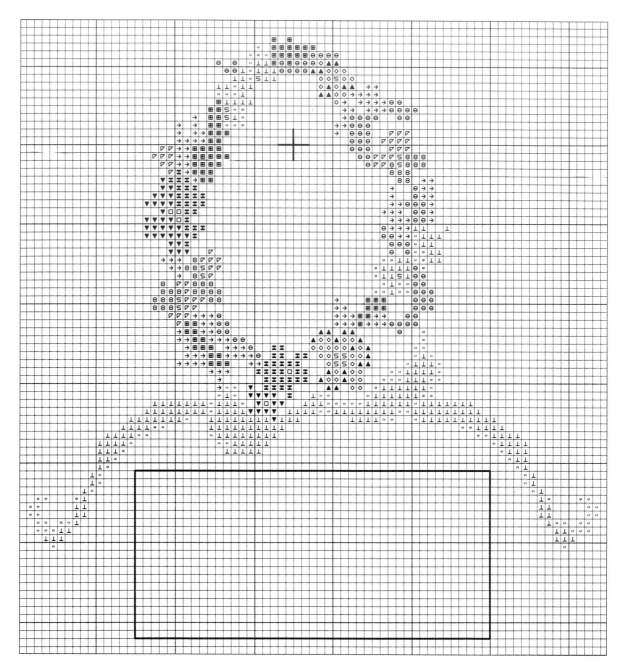

Square Sampler Cross Stitch Chart

Chart Keys

	Spring Variation			Pastel Variation			Spring Variation			Pastel Variation			Spring Variation			Pastel Variation	
	Anchor	DMC		Anchor	DMC		Anchor	DMC		Anchor	DMC		Anchor	DMC		Anchor	DMC
	302	742	5	293	727		11	351	□	1025	347		301	744	▼	4146	950
	118	340	8	129	3325		265	471	⊖	260	772		108	210	▲	74	3354
	120	3747	▽	128	775		254	3348	▣	213	504		110	208	◇	48	818
	68	3687	∘	336	758		266	470	→	262	3363						
	60	605	⊥	1012	754		302	742	⊥	10	351						

~ IRIS PILLOWCASE ~

HARDANGER

BED LINEN

These two projects feature a lovely iris motif, the combination of cross stitch, backstitch and Hardanger creating a delicate but powerful design. The size of the duvet cover may at first seem daunting but it gives you a chance to practice and perfect all the techniques already covered in this chapter.

MATERIALS

Zweigart Linen band (E7272) in white (the length will depend on the size of your pillowcase)

Stranded cottons as listed in the key

Anchor pearl cotton No.5 in white

Tapestry needles size 22 and 24

Sewing thread to stitch the band in place

This lovely pillowcase edging is stitched on a beautiful linen band and if you are feeling adventurous you could embroider the band to fit all the way round the pillowcase. If you want you could fill in the cut out holes with the decorative filling stitches described in Hardanger Techniques page 89.

WORKING THE EMBROIDERY

1 ☒ Find the centre of your linen band and mount it in an embroidery frame or flexi-hoop. Following the chart below, work the cross stitch over two fabric threads using three strands of stranded cotton and a size 24 tapestry needle.

2 ☒ Next stitch the Hardanger as shown on the chart on page 107

using pearl cotton No.5 and size 22 tapestry needle (see Hardanger Techniques page 88). The design can be repeated all the way along the band if you want a more decorative look.

3 ☒ Wash and carefully iron the band face down on a thick, fluffy towel.

4 ☒ Pin, tack, then slipstitch the band neatly into place on the pillowcase edge. Once finished remove the tacking. If you wish to stitch this linen band to fit around the outside of the pillow-case, repeat the design four times, then just extend the Hardanger motifs as much as necessary to fit the pillow.

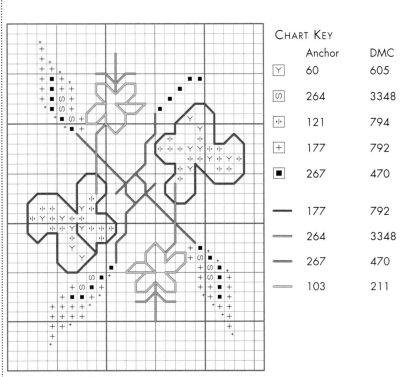

CHART KEY

	Anchor	DMC
Y	60	605
S	264	3348
⁙	121	794
+	177	792
■	267	470
—	177	792
—	264	3348
—	267	470
—	103	211

IRIS PILLOWCASE CROSS STITCH CHART

~ IRIS DUVET COVER ~

MATERIALS
18 count Zweigart Davosa in white, 16in (40cm) full width of fabric (this fits a single duvet cover)

Stranded cottons as listed in the key

Anchor pearl cotton No.5 and No.8 in white

Tapestry needles size 22 and 24

Sewing thread to attach the embroidery to the cover

This design can be easily adapted to fit any size of bed. The full width of the fabric used fits a single duvet, however, it would by easy to fit a larger one by simply joining fabric pieces. The join could be hidden by a pretty ribbon or decorative stitching.

WORKING THE EMBROIDERY

1 ▣ Make sure your strip of fabric fits your duvet cover width and before you start, neaten the edges of the fabric as it frays very easily. When positioning the design, allow 2–3in (6–8cm) at the top and bottom of the fabric for turning.

2 ▣ Mount the fabric in an embroidery frame and begin the Hardanger embroidery a little way in from the selvedge, starting with a waste knot and a long thread (see Cross Stitch basic Techniques page 11). Follow the chart on page 107 and if necessary refer to Hardanger Techniques page 88. Stitch the small dots on the chart as French knots using a size 22 tapestry needle and pearl cotton no.5.

3 ▣ When you have stitched the Hardanger design once you can work out how many hearts you will need to complete the rest of your strip.

4 ▣ Repeat the same process for the row of hearts at the bottom edge of the strip, taking care to align the bottom of the hearts.

When all the embroidery is finished, cut off any waste knots, threading any 'tails' onto a needle and passing the thread through the back of a few stitches.

5 ▣ When you have completed the Hardanger embroidery, wash and then press it face down on a thick, fluffy towel.

6 ▣ The cross stitch iris bouquet is stitched next. The example shown repeats the design five times with a 4in (10cm) gap between each one but you could stitch the design continuously which would make it really sumptuous. Following the chart on page 106 complete the cross stitch and backstitch using three strands of stranded cotton, stitching the cross stitch over two fabric threads.

7 ▣ When you have completed the cross stitching wash the embroidery again and press it face down on a thick, fluffy towel.

8 ▣ You will probably find it easier to pin the embroidery on when the duvet is in the cover, as it is more stable. Turn the edges under, taking care not to pin it to the duvet itself. Tack it firmly in place then slipstitch neatly.

9 ▣ To finish, remove the tacking and press the work again, right side down on a thick, fluffy towel.

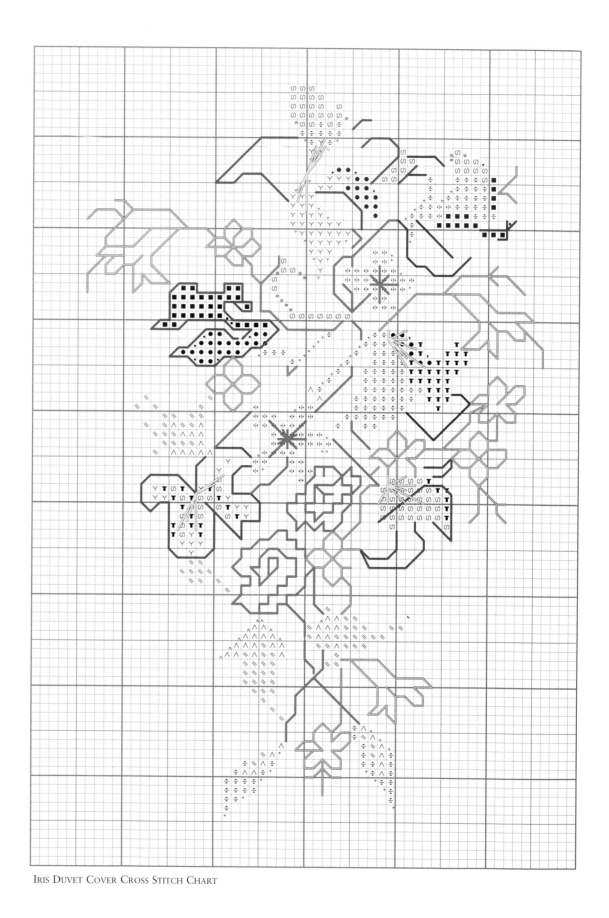

Iris Duvet Cover Cross Stitch Chart

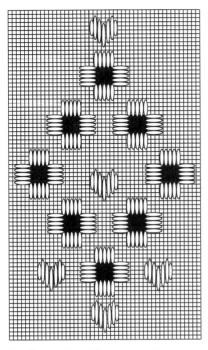

IRIS PILLOW CASE HARDANGER CHART

CROSS STITCH CHART KEY

	Anchor	DMC
∧	267	470
◥	264	3348
Y	1036	824
ᴕ	121	794
÷	177	792
ᛁᛁ	295	727
●	101	550
T	92	3607
■	112	333
—	177	792
—	121	794
—	267	470
—	295	727
—	66	604
—	1036	824
—	264	3348
—	95	3609

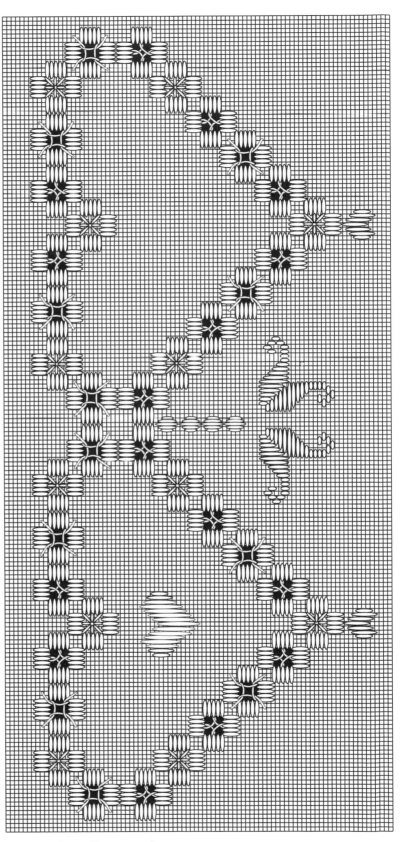

IRIS DUVET COVER HARDANGER CHART

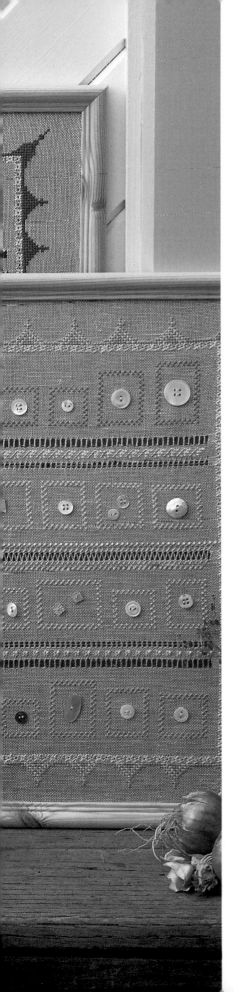

CROSS STITCH PLUS
WITHDRAWN &
PULLED WORK

Ever since strands of natural fibres have been woven to form the warp (the lengthways threads fixed to the loom) and weft (the crossways threads that are interwoven) of a textile, ways have been devised to elaborate and decorate it with embroidery in a beautiful way. An even warp and weft make a fabric admirably suitable for any counted thread work, and withdrawn and pulled work are no exception. At first it is difficult to establish the difference between the various lacy embroideries. One distinction is that withdrawn and pulled work start with a base background fabric, whereas lace is made up of only threads with no original background fabric. The difference between withdrawn and pulled work is subtle but needs to be made clear.

Pulled work is a type of needlework which often uses matching coloured thread and background fabric. The stitches are counted individually and stitched in formation and the thread is pulled tight after every stitch, which creates a little hole or sometimes a ridge, causing the fabric to form a new, interestingly textured pattern. Pulled stitches can be work as borders, as space-filling patterns or built up into geometrical or abstract patterns.

Withdrawn work or drawn thread work is a type of needlework where some of the fabric threads are removed and the remaining threads are counted and stitched over to form a new, lacy pattern. Traditionally a linen fabric is used.

Some of the most dramatic effects in embroidery can be created by altering the surface of fabric in these ways. Removing some of the threads in a fabric always seems to enhance the embroidery making it appear airy, lacy and more intricate. The combination of withdrawn and pulled work with cross stitch may not seem obvious to start with, however, they are all thread processes and you will see what a perfect partnership they make, producing a detailed yet intricately delicate look.

WITHDRAWN & PULLED WORK ◼ BASIC TECHNIQUES

USING A CHART AND WITHDRAWING THREADS

The withdrawn and pulled work stitching instructions are combined with the cross stitch charts. The areas to be stitched with pulled work and withdrawn thread work are indicated by outlined boxes. Withdrawing threads, the fundamental technique in withdrawn work, is foolproof if you follow these simple steps.

1 ◼ First look carefully at the chart you are following and establish the amount of threads to be removed and the area they are to cover which are identified on the charts as rectangular blocks

with a black outline. All the horizontal threads contained *within* an outlined block are the ones to remove. If a project has more than one block, finish each block in turn before moving onto the next. With reference to Figure 1a, pin each end of the area to be withdrawn, marking the correct amount of threads as shown by the chart. Find the middle of that area and put a pin there also.

2 ◼ Take a sharp pair of embroidery scissors and snip through the horizontal threads, as indicated by the middle pin shown on Figure 1b. With the blunt end of a tapestry needle,

wheedle out one cut thread, removing it as far as the appropriate end pin.

3 ◼ Thread this loose end into a tapestry needle and weave it into the edge marked by the side pin shown on Figure 1c. Follow the weave of the fabric by going in and out. Weave through about four to five threads, ending at the back of the work. Snip off closely to the fabric, so no ends show.

4 ◼ Repeat this individually for all the horizontal threads until you have a neat area of vertical threads left to stitch on (see Figure 1d).

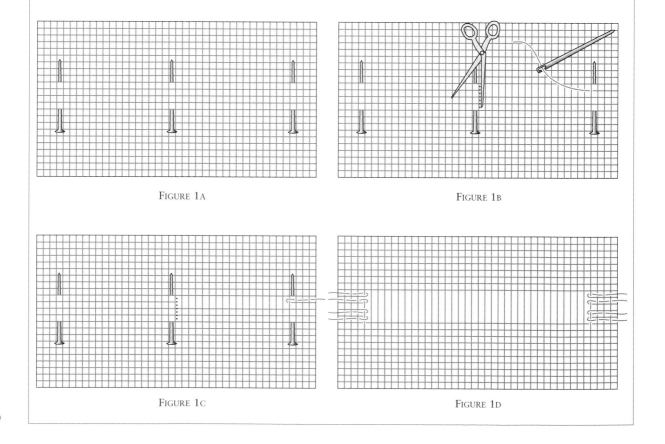

FIGURE 1A

FIGURE 1B

FIGURE 1C

FIGURE 1D

WRAPPED BARS

Wrapped bars are based on satin stitch and may be worked loosely or tightly to create different effects.

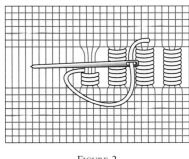

FIGURE 2

1 ⊠ Withdraw the number of fabric threads as indicated by the outlined blocks on the chart you are following (see opposite for how to do this). Then, starting with a waste knot (see page 11) bring the needle out at the bottom right-hand corner of the block four threads in, ready to start the first bar (see Figure 2).

2 ⊠ The stitching is now done on the fabric threads that have not been removed. Start on the right

side, pick up four threads and wrap the yarn over and over, creating regular stitches until the top is reached and a bar is formed (see Figure 2).

3 ⊠ Now carry the yarn over to the next four fabric threads and wrap the stitches over and over until the bottom is reached. Continue along the row until the end. Fasten off by passing the thread through one of the bars using a sharp embroidery needle.

INTERLACING STITCH

This stitch is made over groups of open fabric threads. Once the stitch is started you must complete the row all in one go to keep the tension even. The stitch is made through the middle of the fabric threads that remain in place when the others are withdrawn. It does not attach itself to the fabric apart from at each end of the row.

1 ⊠ First withdraw the number of fabric threads as indicated by the outlined blocks on the chart (see Using a Chart and Withdrawing Threads opposite).

2 ⊠ Using a long waste knot to start (see page 11), begin at the right-hand side (or from the left-hand side if you are left-handed) and bring the needle up through the fabric as indicated in figure 3a.

3 ⊠ Count four fabric threads as in Figure 3a. Insert the needle under two threads and up between the two pairs of threads so that

the needle is positioned over the second pair of threads as shown in Figure 3b. Do not pull your needle through the work.

4 ⊠ Now, without removing the needle from these threads, twist the needle until it faces the other way. The threads will automatically twist as you do this (see Figure 3c).

5 ⊠ Pinch your fingers together over this stitch and pull the needle gently through, keeping the thread horizontal and taut. Repeat this process all the way down the row (see Figure 3d) and fasten off securely into the fabric edge.

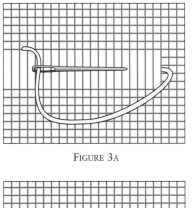

FIGURE 3A

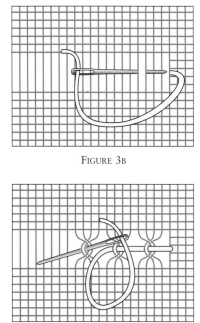

FIGURE 3B

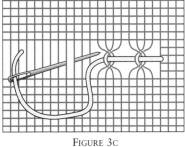

FIGURE 3C

FIGURE 3D

ZIGZAG HEMMING STITCH

This linear stitch forms a simple geometric pattern which creates an effective border.

1 ⊠ First, withdraw the number of fabric threads as indicated on the chart you are following (see Withdrawing Threads page 110).

2 ⊠ Use a waste knot to start (see page 11) and work the stitch from left to right, beginning with the bottom row. Bring the needle out at the arrow shown on Figure 4a and use it to pick up four of the fabric threads left after the withdrawing of threads. The needle should pass behind and round as shown in Figure 4a.

3 ⊠ Take the needle down to emerge at the front of the fabric, four threads to the right (see Figure 4b). This completes one stitch. Continue to the end.

4 ⊠ Stitch the top row in the same way as the bottom row, first turning your work 180° (upside-down). When you stitch the top row, take four fabric threads as before but split the bottom row in half – this forms the zigzag pattern as shown in Figure 4c. Fasten off securely, using a sharp embroidery needle to make this as invisible as possible.

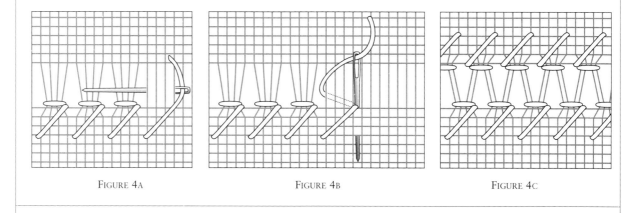

FIGURE 4A   FIGURE 4B   FIGURE 4C

WAVE STITCH

This pulled stitch is quick to work and useful for filling and covering background areas. We have worked the stitch from right to left.

1 ⊠ Using a waste knot to start (see page 11), bring the needle up through the fabric at the point indicated by the arrow on Figure 5a. Count two fabric threads to the right and four threads down and insert the needle at point A shown on Figure 5a. This forms a diagonal stitch. Now bring the needle out at point B (this is four fabric threads left of point A). Take the needle back to the arrow point and bring it out four threads left of this to point C. Each stitch should be pulled so the holes that form will alternate.

2 ⊠ Repeat this pattern of stitching to the end of the row and then continue to stitch more rows (see Figure 5b). When you need to fasten off, make sure the thread can't be seen through the hole – a sharp embroidery needle will help.

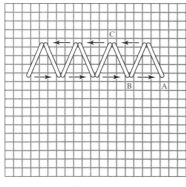

FIGURE 5A

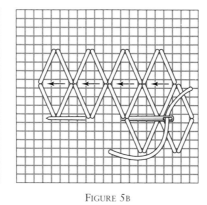

FIGURE 5B

RINGED BACKSTITCH

This is a pulled stitch, worked in backstitch in a figure-eight movement from left to right. It is important to pull every stitch tighter than you normally would.

1 ▣ Use a waste knot to start the first journey or row (see page 11). Bring the needle out at point (1) shown on Figure 6a, then insert it back into the fabric at a point two threads to the right and two up (2). Repeat this stitch again over the top of the first stitch.

2 ▣ Now bring the needle out four fabric threads to the left and two threads down (3). Take the needle back to the arrow (1). Repeat this stitch again over the top. The next stitch is four threads to the left and two threads up (4), which will create a backstitch to the last stitch. Repeat over the top. Continue to the end making sure every stitch is done twice (see Figure 6a).

3 ▣ Now start the second journey or row. Turn the work 180° (upside-down) and repeat steps 1 and 2 above (see Figure 6b). You will notice that some of the stitches overlap to create four stitches – this is correct but has not been shown in the diagram as it is too complicated to represent accurately. Fasten off securely through the back of the work as invisibly as possible – a sharp embroidery needle will help.

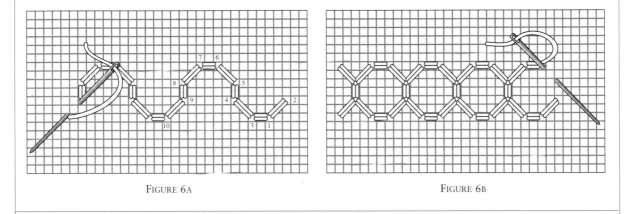

FIGURE 6A   FIGURE 6B

THREE-SIDED STITCH

This is a pulled work stitch that travels from right to left. Each stitch needs to be pulled tightly.

1 ▣ Use a waste knot to start (see page 11) and bring the needle out at the arrow point shown on Figure 7. Put the needle back in four fabric threads to the right at point A and then bring it back to the arrow point. Repeat this stitch again over the top of the first stitch.

2 ▣ Following Figure 7, count four fabric threads up and two threads to the right and insert the needle at point B. Return to the arrow point and repeat this stitch again over the top of the last. Insert the needle at point C and then bring it up four fabric

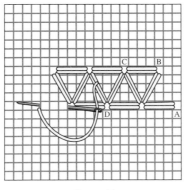

FIGURE 7

threads to the right at point B. Repeat this stitch again.

3 ▣ Take your needle back to point C, and then back diagonally to the arrow point. Complete this stitch again. You are now back at the arrow. Take your needle under four threads to the left to point D. The stitch is now repeated.

4 ▣ Continue along the row in this fashion, so each stitch has two stitches to it. Fasten off securely on the back of the work, as invisibly as possible – a sharp embroidery needle will help you.

EYELET STITCH

Eyelet stitches are a form of satin stitch where all the stitches converge on a central hole.

1 ⊠ Use a waste knot to start (see page 11) and bring the needle up to the front at a corner point.

2 ⊠ Starting from a corner, work each stitch in succession. Figure 4 page 89 shows the direction of the stitches into the centre. Giving an extra tug as you complete each stitch will produce a more pleasing effect overall, as a neat hole will be formed.

3 ⊠ Fasten off the thread by securing it under the back of surrounding stitches, or pass the thread through the back of the work to start another filling stitch.

STAR FILLING STITCH

This is a surface filling stitch which is very effective. It consists of a series of cross stitches worked on top of each other.

1 ⊠ Use a waste knot to start (see page 11) and make a cross with one vertical stitch and one horizontal stitch (see Figure 8a).

2 ⊠ Place a diagonal cross stitch on top (see Figure 8b) and anchor this with a smaller cross on top (see Figure 8c). Fasten off with a small stitch on the back.

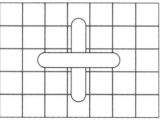

FIGURE 8A

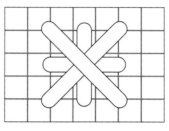

FIGURE 8B

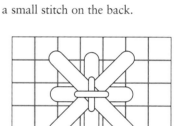

FIGURE 8C

WITHDRAWN & PULLED WORK ⊠ TOOLS OF THE TRADE

FABRIC

It is very important that the fabric used in withdrawn and pulled work be of an even weave nature and not that of an Aida. Aida has been heat set at the various inter-junctions and so individual threads cannot be withdrawn or pulled with success. The more open evenweave fabrics are easier to pull and stitch. A pure linen is the most traditional of back-ground fabrics for this embroidery and is also perfect for cross stitch.

NEEDLES

It is useful to have an embroidery needle (size 7–9) for fastening off the ends of the threads in withdrawn embroidery to ensure a secure finish.

WATER-SOLUBLE PEN

You will find a water-soluble pen useful, particularly for the Collection Sampler project, as it allows you to mark a design. The marks fade when sprayed or dampened with water. It is best to test the pen on a piece of scrap fabric before using on a specific project.

~ CHERRY TABLE-MATS ~

STARTING TO PULL

These striking table-mats are an ideal introduction to pulled work, combining it with cross stitch in a most attractive way. The mats are easy to stitch; there is no withdrawn thread work required, only mastery of a pulled stitch called wave stitch. The pulled work area is in the centre of the design and is marked off on the chart, showing you exactly where to stitch.

MATERIALS
20 count Zweigart Bellana fabric in sage green, 12in (30.5cm) square

Stranded cottons as listed in the key

Pearl cotton No.5 in Anchor 875 (or DMC 1206)

Tapestry needle size 22 and sharps embroidery needle size 7

These pretty mats would be perfect for any surface top which needed an extra bit of decoration. They would also be ideal for placing under a vase of flowers or perhaps with your favourite perfume bottle on. There are two colour versions for you to choose from, the bright red cherry one being ideal for a sunny kitchen or the more subtle pink cherry one for a bedroom.

WORKING THE EMBROIDERY

1 ⊠ Mount the fabric in a hoop or frame and following the chart on page 16, having chosen a colour version, start with a waste knot. Count from the centre of the chart to the cross stitching area (see Cross Stitch Basic Techniques page 10). Use a size 22 tapestry needle and three strands of stranded cotton and work the cross stitch over two fabric threads.

2 ⊠ Once the cross stitch is complete you can begin the pulled work section in the central panel. This is marked on the chart as an outlined box. Check your fabric is still tightly tensioned in your frame before you start to work. Using the pearl cotton No.5 and a size 22 tapestry needle, start the first row of wave stitch at the top right-hand corner of the box and work from right to left (see Withdrawn and Pulled Work Techniques page 12 for how to wave stitch). Once the first row is complete, move down and work the row beneath, and so on. Fasten off the thread using a sharps embroidery needle.

3 ⊠ When you have finished all the stitching, carefully wash and press the embroidered piece face down on a fluffy towel.

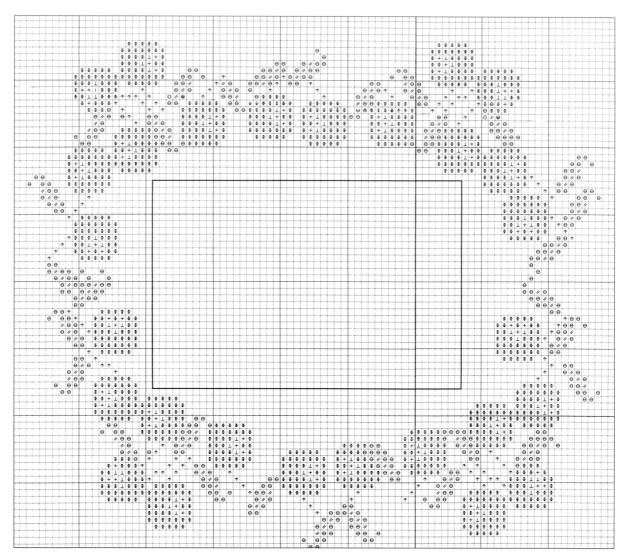

CHERRY TABLE-MATS CHART

MAKING UP THE TABLE-MATS

4 ⊠ Turn all four edges of the
embroidered mat under twice to
neaten. Pin and tack them to hold
the edges in place. Using a pearl
cotton No.5 and a size 22 needle,
blanket stitch around the edge (see
Cross Stitch Basic Techniques page
9). Take extra care when you stitch
around the corners and remove the
pins and tacking when finished. We
added tassels as decoration (see
Finishing Techniques page 126
for making tassels).

CHART KEY FOR RED CHERRIES

	Anchor	DMC
‡	1028	498
+	13	347
⊥	39	309
⊖	212	561
⁄⁄	876	502
↑	861	3362

CHART KEY FOR PINK CHERRIES

	Anchor	DMC
‡	77	3687
+	895	3733
⊥	894	776
⊖	843	3012
⁄⁄	1043	369
↑	214	966

~ STAMP AND BUTTON SAMPLERS ~

COLLECTION

SAMPLERS

These two samplers have been especially designed for your personal collection of treasured objects which you wish to display. Working one or both of them will give you a superb introduction to withdrawn work and further develop your pulled work skills. The withdrawn work is positioned in five blocks across each sampler, making an effective addition to each design. Three different pulled work stitches are then used to decorate these panels. Combining cross stitch with withdrawn embroidery in this way gives these samplers a wonderful contemporary feel.

MATERIALS

28 count Zweigart Cashel Linen in oatmeal, 20 x 24in (51 x 61cm)

Stranded cottons as listed in the key

Tapestry needle size 24

A water-soluble pen

These collection samplers have two colour variations – one bold and bright, the other soft and subtle – so you can pick the one that most enhances your collection of objects. Obviously your collection will vary in size from the ones shown here, but the samplers are easy to adapt, allowing you to create a unique work at the same time as being fun to stitch. Why not stitch one featuring Brownie badges or football cards – the possibilities are endless.

WORKING THE EMBROIDERY

1 ⊠ Mount the fabric in a hoop or frame and using a waste knot to start, follow the chart on pages 120–121 (see Cross Stitch Basic Techniques page 11). Begin by working the outer cross stitch border using a size 24 tapestry needle and three strands of stranded cotton over two fabric threads.

2 ⊠ When the cross stitch is complete, stitch the inner border of eyelet stitches (see Withdrawn and Pulled Work Techniques page 114). These are indicated on the chart as blocks of nine cross stitch symbols (two different sorts) in the appropriate colour. To distinguish

the eyelets from cross stitches, these blocks have been outlined with a thin black line but the line is *not* to be stitched. Use three strands of stranded cotton and a size 24 needle for these eyelet stitches.

3 ⊠ Next work the areas of withdrawn thread embroidery (blocks A–E on the chart). Start and finish each block separately as this will keep the fabric more stable while stitching. Begin by withdrawing the threads on block A. The number of horizontal fabric threads to be removed are shown within the outlines of the blocks A–E on the main chart. See Withdrawn and Pulled Work Techniques on page 110 for how to withdraw threads.

4 ⊠ Once the threads have been withdrawn on a block you can complete the stitching. The stitches for each block are indicated by the key on page 121 – for example, block A is a row of wrapped bars. See Withdrawn and Pulled Work Techniques on page 111 for how to work the relevant stitches. All the stitches within the blocks use three strands of stranded cotton and a size 24 tapestry needle.

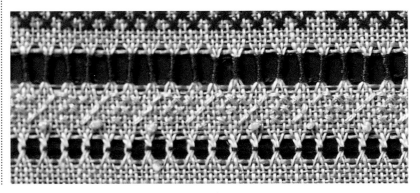

5 ▣ Once all the stitching is complete you will see that there are blank sections left on the sampler for your collection of objects. Lay your items on the sampler, spacing them out. Take a bit of time over this to ensure you are happy with the positioning

of all your objects.

6 ▣ With a water-soluble pen draw around each object making a border line – you will need to judge the distance from the object by eye, depending on your object. Before removing your collection pieces it is a good idea at this stage to make a note of where each item goes.

7 ▣ Remove your objects and, using a size 24 tapestry needle and three strands of stranded cotton over two fabric threads, cross stitch on the drawn line. Using the chart as a reference, add another cross stitch border around this first one, so a double border is formed.

8 ▣ Wash and press your work face down on a thick, fluffy towel.

9 ▣ Stitch the objects back on your sampler. Select a coloured mount board, choosing the best colour for your collection. Refer to page 126 to finish and frame your piece.

A chart is provided for the stamp sampler on pages 120–121, but you could stitch a sampler in any colours to suit the decor of your room or the collection you wish to display, as the alternative sampler pictured here shows.

To stitch the button sampler the following colours were used: Anchor 2, 338, 292, 158, 337, 25, 1012, 103; DMC Blanc, 356, 3078, 828, 3778, 963, 948, 211

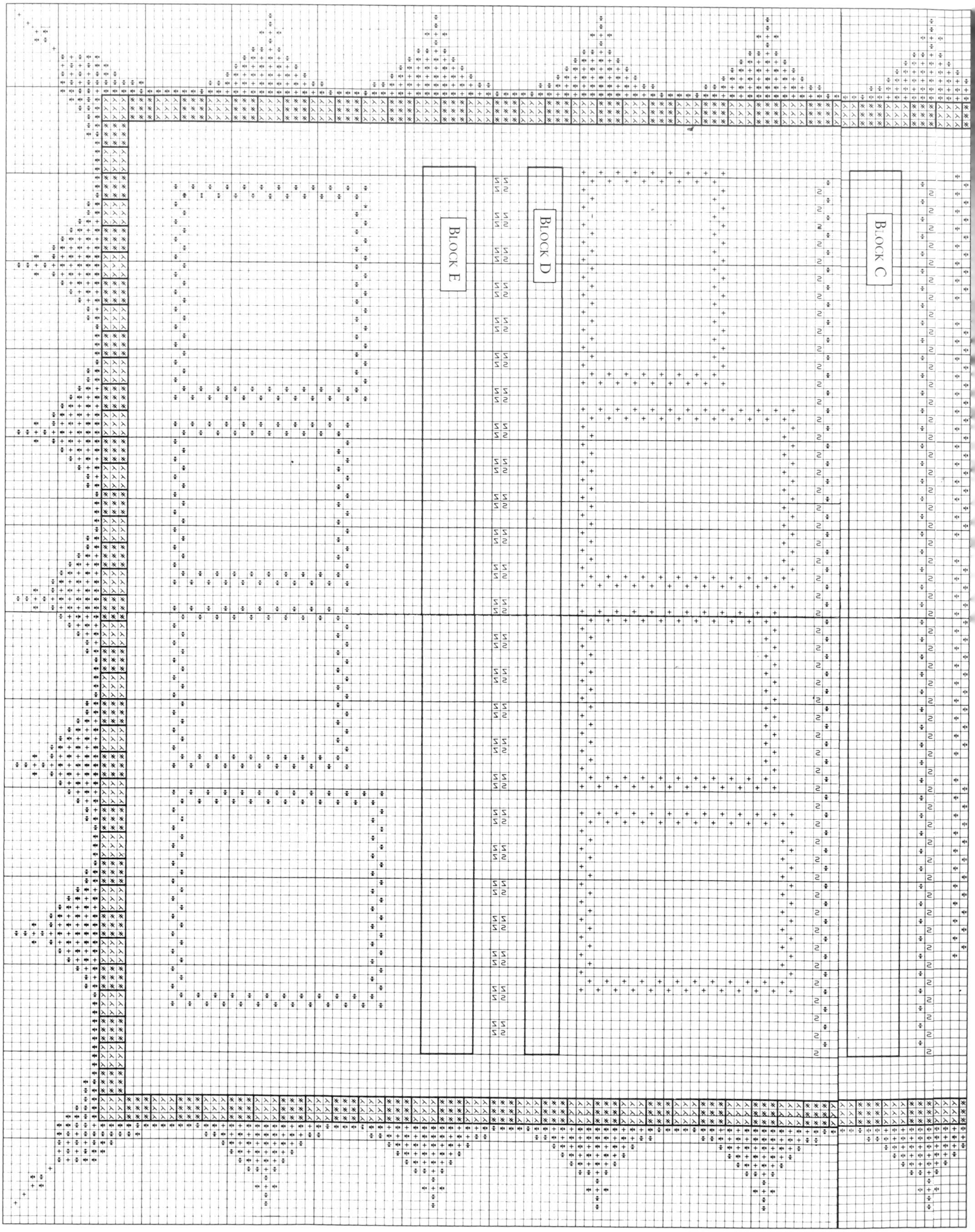

BLOCK E

BLOCK D

BLOCK C

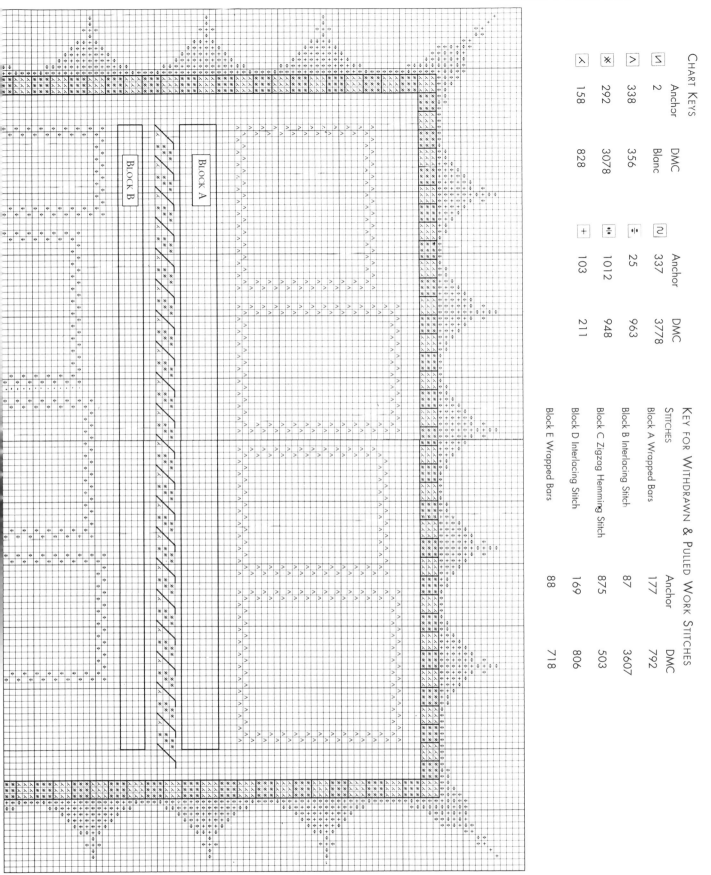

CHART KEYS

	Anchor	DMC		Anchor	DMC
⊠	2	Blanc	⊡	337	3778
⋏	338	356	⊡	25	963
⋇	292	3078	⊡	1012	948
⋏	158	828	+	103	211

KEY FOR WITHDRAWN & PULLED WORK STITCHES

STITCHES	Anchor	DMC	Anchor	DMC
Block A Wrapped Bars	177	792		
Block B Interlacing Stitch	87	3607		
Block C Zigzag Hemming Stitch	875	503		
Block D Interlacing Stitch	169	806		
Block E Wrapped Bars	88	718		

COMBINED

STITCHES

This beautiful advanced project uses all the skills learnt in this chapter on withdrawn work and pulled embroidery, allowing you to practise them further. In addition it gives you the chance to learn some new stitches. This versatile design could be altered easily to make a square cushion or even a panel for a bolster cushion.

MATERIALS

28 count Zweigart Quaker (Evenweave) fabric in biscuit, 12 x 23in (30.5 x 58.5cm)

Stranded cottons as listed in the key

Tapestry needle size 24

Coloured lining fabric of your choice

Backing fabric of your choice

A strip of iron-on Vilene

Bell-pull ends of your choice, 6in (15cm)

This bell-pull would be ideal for any stairway, hall or traditionally placed at the side of a fireplace. The lacy embroidery combined with cross stitch gives it a sophisticated look.

WORKING THE EMBROIDERY

1 ▨ Mount the fabric into a frame, leaving 4in (10cm) at the top and 3½in (9cm) in from one side before you start to stitch. This will ensure that the bell-pull is spaced correctly on the fabric and allow you to finish the bell-pull neatly once the embroidery is completed.

2 ▨ Use a waste knot with a long thread to start (see Cross Stitch Basic Techniques page 11) and beginning at the top of the chart on pages 124–125 work the first cross stitch row. Use a size 24 tapestry needle and three strands of stranded cotton over two fabric threads for all the cross stitch. Work your way down the chart – it is your choice whether to work all the cross stitch first or alternate it with the withdrawn and pulled work blocks.

3 ▨ To work the areas of withdrawn thread embroidery (blocks A–J on the chart), it is best to start and finish each block separately as this will keep the fabric more stable while stitching. Begin by withdrawing the threads on block A. The number of fabric threads to be removed are shown within the outlines of the blocks A–J on the chart. See Withdrawn and Pulled Work Techniques on page 110 for how to withdraw threads.

4 ▨ Once the threads have been withdrawn on a block you can complete the stitching. The stitches and colours for each block are indicated by the special key on page 124 – for example, block A is zigzag hemming stitch. See Withdrawn and Pulled Work Techniques on page 111 for how to work the relevant stitches. All the stitches within the blocks use three strands of stranded cotton and a size 24 tapestry needle.

5 ▨ When you have completed all the stitching, wash and carefully press the embroidered piece face down on a fluffy towel.

6 ▨ To line the bell-pull with the coloured fabric of your choice, first iron the strip of iron-on Vilene to the reverse of this fabric. This will be the size of your chosen bell-pull. Place this right sides down to the wrong side of the bell-pull, so that when you hold it up you can see the fabric through the lacy embroidery. Pin and tack this place.

7 ▨ Fold the sides of the bell-pull over the back of the inside fabric and press gently. Then attach the bell-pull ends at the top and bottom.

8 ▨ Place the piece of backing fabric on the back of the bell-pull, turning all four raw edges under neatly. Pin, tack and slipstitch this to the back to hide any raw edges and finish off neatly. Remove all pins and tacking stitches.

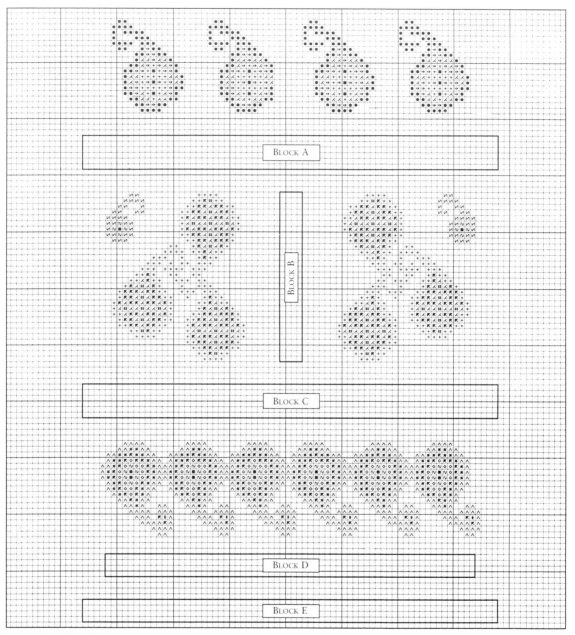

PAISLEY BELL-PULL CHART (TOP)

CHART KEY FOR WITHDRAWN AND PULLED WORK STITCHES

	Anchor	DMC		Anchor	DMC
Block A Zigzag Hemming Stitch	152	939	Block F Eyelet Stitch	300	745
Block B Wrapped Bars (horizontal)	47	321	Block G Ringed Backstitch	269	936
Block C Ringed Backstitch	941	793	Block H Wrapped Bars	339	920
Block D Interlacing Stitch	136	799	Block I Star Filling Stitch	281	732
Block E Three-sided Stitch	267	470	Block J Zigzag Hemming Stitch	65	3350

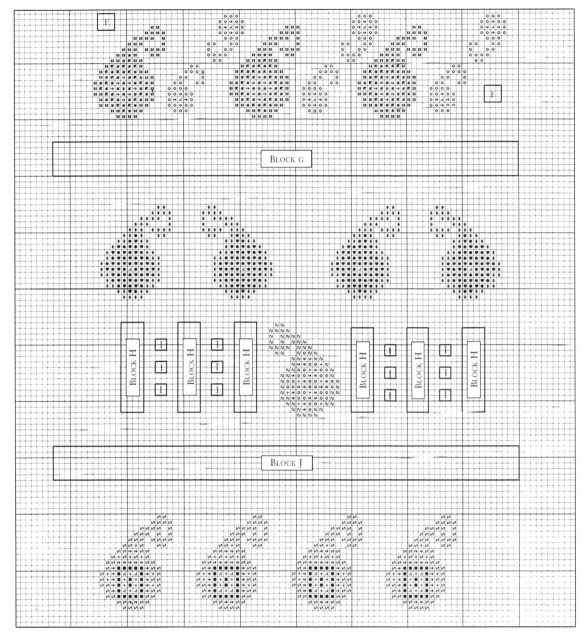

PAISLEY BELL-PULL CHART (BOTTOM)

CHART KEY FOR CROSS STITCH

	Anchor	DMC			Anchor	DMC			Anchor	DMC
⋉	339	920		⩧	941	793		◇	65	3350
⋀	281	732		•¦•	300	745		●	1006	349
⊠	269	936		+	136	799		H	47	321
⋋	262	3363		◤	362	437		■	13	347
⋈	289	307		♥	366	739				

▣ FINISHING TECHNIQUES ▣

WASHING & PRESSING WORK

It may be necessary to wash the complete embroidery in lukewarm water and a little hand-wash detergent. Place it as flat as possible in a bowl and gently agitate with the fingers to loosen any marks. Rinse in the same way and place flat between two towels. When almost dry, place the piece over a thick towel face down and press the reverse with a medium iron.

Extra care should be taken when ironing a piece of work that includes metallic threads and blending filaments. Always use a pressing cloth to separate the iron from the back of the embroidery.

We do not recommend washing and pressing silk ribbon work as the stitches are likely to squash.

USING IRON-ON INTERFACING

Iron-on interfacing such as Vilene. It can be useful when mounting pieces in small objects to stop the cut edges fraying. Cut the inter-facing, to size if required and place it shiny side down over the reverse of the work. Press, using a medium iron, into a thick fluffy towel, for ten to fifteen seconds. Test one of the corners, if the interfacing still peels away, hold the iron over it a little longer until it is securely glued. Trim the work as necessary.

STRETCHING & MOUNTING FOR FRAMING

If having a picture framed professionally, you should always check that the framer laces and stretches the work – if they mention glue or sticky backing board, go somewhere else. To mount your work yourself buy some acid-free mounting board, in a colour that will not show through the embroidery. Cut the mounting board to fit inside your picture frame, remembering to allow for the thickness of fabric pulled over the edges of the board.

Place the cut board on the reverse of the work in the position you require. Starting from the centre of one of the longest edges, fold the fabric over the board and pin through the fabric and into the edge of the board to keep the fabric from moving. Keep checking that it is in the correct place and that there are no wrinkles or bumps.

Working from the centre, using long lengths of a very strong thread lace back-wards and forwards across the gap (see Figure 11a). Remove the pins.

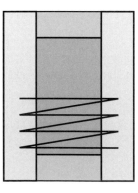

FIGURE 11A

Repeat this process for the shorter sides, taking care to fold the corners in neatly (Figure 11b).

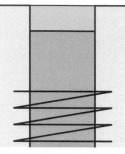

FIGURE 11B

MOUNTING WORK IN A FOOTSTOOL

Put the cushion pad of the footstool, padded side down, centrally on top of the wrong side of the work. Lift the sides of the work around to the back of the pad, checking that the pad is still centrally placed.

Using a long length of strong cotton thread, thread a stitch in the centre of one of the sides. Pull half of the long thread through leaving a long end hanging. Lace up one side of the stool but do not pull the stitches tight yet. Lace up the other side with the long thread that you left, checking that the embroidery is positioned correctly. Pull the lacing taut and fasten the thread securely.

Fold the top and bottom edges over the lacing and tuck the fabric under so that it forms neat corners when viewed from the front of the work. Using another long length of thread make a stitch in the centre of the top edge and repeat the lacing as for the first two sides.

Mount the laced pad in the footstool and secure with the underside screws.

MOUNTING WORK IN A CARD

Ready-made card mounts are pre-folded and have three sections, the middle one having a window for your embroidery.

First check that your embroidery fits and looks good within the window space. Put your embroidery on top of the window section and trim the excess fabric to within that third.

Put small lengths of double-sided adhesive tape around the window area. Remove the backing from the tape. Lay the card on top of the embroidery so that it shows neatly through the window. Press into place. A bit of extra tape may be needed at the top and bottom to secure the fabric.

Fold the third of the card to cover the back of the embroidery, making sure that the card opens correctly before securing with double-sided adhesive tape.

MAKING A TASSEL

Decide on the tassel length required. Cut a piece of stiff card in a square to this size. Wrap the thread round and round the card (see Figure 12a). This forms the body of the tassel, so make it as fat as you like.

Cut across the threads, as shown whilst holding tightly to the tassel at the top.

Take the tassel off the card and pinch the threads together, then tightly wrap a length of thread just below the loop at the top (see Figure 12b). Knot this and thread the ends through to join the other lengths. If your tassel edges are uneven, trim them. Do this by rolling the tassel firmly in a piece of paper in a cigarette fashion and cut through in a straight line near the bottom of the tassel ends.

To attach the finished tassel use a length of matching thread through the loop at the top.

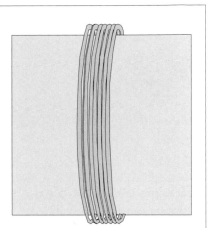

FIGURE 12A

FIGURE 12B

SUPPLIERS

The following companies can be contacted for further information about the materials used in this book.

◩ For your nearest stockist of Zweigart fabrics including Aida Plus and waste canvas:
DMC, Pullman Road, Wigston, Leicestershire LE18 2DY
Tel: 0116 2811040

◩ For your nearest stockist of threads:
Coats Crafts UK, PO Box 22, The Lingfield Estate, McMullen Road, Darlington DL1 1YQ
Tel: 01325 381010

◩ For your nearest stockist of Caron threads:
MacLeod Craft Marketing, West Yonderton, Warlock Road, Bridge of Weir, Renfrewshire PA11 3SR
Tel: 01505 612 618

◩ For Trimit beads:
Spoilt for Choice, 35 March Road, Wimblington, March, Cambridgeshire PE15 0RW
Tel: 01354 740341

◩ For silk ribbon:
Ribbon Designs, 42 Lake View, Edgware, Middlesex HA8 7RU
Tel: 0181 9584966

◩ For beads, brooches, beading needles, paperweights and notepaper block:
Framecraft Miniatures Ltd, 372–76 Summer Lane, Hockley, Birmingham B19 3QA
Tel: 0121 2120551

◩ For the tapestry slipper kit:
Fancy Footwork Ltd, 90 Gore Road, Hackney, London E9 7HW
Tel: 0181 9855193

◩ For the dressing gown, camisole top, duvet cover and pillowcase contact your local branch of Marks & Spencer.

◩ For the footstool and for framing:
Woodhouse, Rock Channel, Rye, East Sussex TN31 7HJ
Tel: 01797 225145

◩ For three-fold card mounts:
Impress, Slough Farm, Westhall, Suffolk IP19 8RN
Tel: 01986 781422

◩ For your nearest stockist of embroidery scissors:
Simply Scissors, 48 Midholm, London NW11 6LN
Tel: 0181 4584814

◼ INDEX ◼